a
time to die
and
a
time to live

Books by Eric Bentley

a
time to die
and
a
time to live

two short plays

by Eric Bentley

GROVE PRESS, INC.
NEW YORK

acknowledgments

I want to thank all those who have given their time to these plays, thus helping me, I believe, to improve them. Isaiah Sheffer was the first director to work on either script. He produced and directed an early draft of *A Time to Die* on radio (WEVD, New York City), and he experimented with the same play in a workshop at Columbia University. Edward Thommen directed the plays at the Provincetown Theatre on the Wharf in the summer of 1967.

Herbert Berghof and Uta Hagen first staged the plays as a pair. Their production made me see certain limitations in the text and forced me to prepare the very different versions of both plays published here. I am dedicating *A Time to Live* to them because this was their joint effort, Miss Hagen lending her sensitive hand to the direction, and Mr. Berghof painting an unforgettable portrait of Peleus.

ERIC BENTLEY
Summer 1968

The two plays were first produced, in an earlier version, under the title *Commitments: Two Plays for One Evening* on Monday, March 27, 1967, at the HB Playwrights Theater, 124 Bank Street, New York City, the first one directed by Herbert Berghof, the second by Uta Hagen, both designed by Lester Polakov, with the following cast (where two names are given for one role, it means that one actor played the role at certain performances, the other at others):

a time to die

FIRST SLAVE	Oliver Berg Don Bishop
SECOND SLAVE	Richard Morse William Traylor
ANTIGONE	Olga Bellin Josephine Lemmo
CREON	Arthur Hill James Patterson

In this production, all other roles were played by First Slave and Second Slave.

a time to live

PELEUS	Herbert Berghof Salem Ludwig
PYRRHUS	Michael Holmes George Welbes
ANDROMACHE	Beverly Luckenbach Fern Sloan
HERMIONE	Joanne Bayes Shirley Cox
MENELAUS	Edward Morehouse Augustus Sultatos
ORESTES	Kent Broadhurst Angus M. Duncan
AGAMEMNON	Michael Higgins Fritz Weaver

a
time to die

For Michael

The following acts are representative of violations of the law of war ("war crimes"):

a. ...
b. ...
c. Maltreatment of dead bodies.

—General Maxwell D. Taylor, "The Law of Land Warfare," *U.S. Army Field Manual 27–10*.

PROLOGUE

Many indeed are this world's wonders
　　And none more wonderful than Creon.
With plow and spade the soil he sunders,
　　Galleys he builds to sail the sea on.

No fish is safe from him; no bird
　　Escape from Creon's nets can find.
Ox, camel, horse have all deferred
　　To his unconquerable mind.

Words he maneuvers and can get
　　Thousands of men to fight and win.
The one thing he's not mastered yet
　　Is singular and feminine.

CHARACTERS

ANTIGONE, *aged 16*
CREON, *aged 40*
TUTOR, *youngish*
HAEMON, *aged 20*
OFFICER
SOLDIER
TIRESIAS, *aged 90*
TWO SLAVES *who tell the story*

In or near Thebes.

FIRST SLAVE: Antigone is dead. Dead at sixteen. She decided to die, and she died.

SECOND SLAVE: We shall show you how she reached this decision. We who were her slaves.

FIRST SLAVE: It began with her father whom we served before her, and his answer to the Sphinx's riddle, which was: "Man."

SECOND SLAVE: "Man's fate is Man himself," said Oedipus.

FIRST SLAVE: The priests gave way but bided their time.

SECOND SLAVE: They knew about the parricide and the incest.

FIRST SLAVE: The plague, they said, was a curse upon the parricidal and incestuous king.

SECOND SLAVE: It would stop if and when he destroyed himself.

FIRST SLAVE: Oedipus put his eyes out and fled Thebes. But the plague did not stop.

SECOND SLAVE: Creon stepped into Oedipus' place.

FIRST SLAVE: He did not ask the plague to end.

SECOND SLAVE: He ended it. And not by sanctity, but by sanitation.

FIRST SLAVE: He quarantined the sick and had Thebes washed from one end to the other.

SECOND SLAVE: The plague died out. The priests went into exile.

FIRST SLAVE: Creon was Regent, for Polynices, Oedipus' son, was still a child.

SECOND SLAVE: And Creon cut in the stone above the city gate the words: "Man's fate is Man."

Gong.

FIRST SLAVE: But what is Man? People like us—and the others. Well-meaning cities like ours—and foreign cities, breathing fire and brimstone. Man is Thebes; but Man is also Argos.

SECOND SLAVE: And on the day when Polynices came of age and would have been crowned, Argos declared war.

FIRST SLAVE: Polynices trembled. He had no plan for the defense of the city. Creon swept him aside and undertook the defense of the city himself.

SECOND SLAVE: And Creon the Regent became King Creon.

FIRST SLAVE: Polynices fled.

SECOND SLAVE: To Argos.

FIRST SLAVE: And war raged on the Theban plain.

Gong.

SECOND SLAVE: In these same years the child Antigone grew up.

FIRST SLAVE: She had been too small and perhaps too frail to go with Oedipus when he left Thebes.

SECOND SLAVE: Creon raised her, was a second father to her, and stood between her and embattled Thebes.

FIRST SLAVE: A wing of the royal palace became hers with its own colonnade and gardens: they too stood between her and embattled Thebes.

SECOND SLAVE: One day, soon after her sixteenth birthday, Antigone's Tutor brought her a message.

Gong.

I

The colonnade. ANTIGONE. *To her, the* TUTOR.

TUTOR: Creon asked me to talk to you.

ANTIGONE: Oh? Why didn't he come himself? He always comes to the colonnade in the afternoon. Almost every day . . .

TUTOR: Antigone, there has been a battle. Yesterday. News is still coming in . . .

ANTIGONE: You turn pale. What is it? Did we lose?

TUTOR: No, no, it's not that. We won. We won a great victory . . .

ANTIGONE: A great victory is great news! Why isn't Creon here to give it to me?

TUTOR: The news *is* great for Thebes, but someone near to you fought on the other side . . .

ANTIGONE: My brother Polynices . . .

TUTOR: He fell in battle. Creon asked me to tell you.

ANTIGONE: He fell? Yesterday? *(Pause.)* Poor, poor Polynices! *(Pause.)* How did he die?

TUTOR: The King of Argos had placed him at the head of the whole Argive army . . . Now, since their losses were very heavy . . .

ANTIGONE: Well, where is the body now? Has it been brought to Thebes yet?

TUTOR: Antigone, let me tell my story. No, the body has not been brought to Thebes. Will not be brought to Thebes . . .

ANTIGONE: Don't tell me he's been buried out there on the plain?

TUTOR: No, he . . .

ANTIGONE: No? Then he can still be brought home, he *must* be . . .

TUTOR: Antigone, let me finish. My message is a painful one for you, and I am trying, as Creon instructed me, to soften the blow. To soften both blows.

ANTIGONE: *Both* blows?

TUTOR: Not only is your brother dead. He is not entitled to the rites of burial. Neither in Thebes nor Argos nor any other Greek city have traitors the right to be buried.

ANTIGONE: Traitors! This is the son of Oedipus! Creon cannot treat his own nephew as a common traitor!

TUTOR: He fought for Argos.

ANTIGONE: What place was there for him here? So he ran off to another city!

TUTOR: Argos is not just another city. It is *the* other city, which has taken the other road into the human future. Call it, rather, the inhuman future, for to the Argives that City of Man which Oedipus and Creon both have yearned for is a chimera, an impossible dream. Argos has quite a different goal. Can you guess what? (*Pause.*) The conquest of all Greece.

ANTIGONE: I don't know about politics.

TUTOR: All Greece is to be under the Argive heel. And what a heel! Can you imagine how one prepares for universal conquest?

ANTIGONE: One must be very tyrannical?

TUTOR: One creates a city of soldiers, informers, secret agents, police, and more police. Argos doesn't have law courts, it has military tribunals. Argos doesn't make war just on foreigners: thousands of Argives have already been executed. Argos is no longer a city of men. It is a machine with a single function: conquest.

ANTIGONE: Why are you telling me all this? I only asked . . .

TUTOR: If your brother could be buried. I said no, traitors forfeit the right of burial. You said your brother would be an exception, he was Creon's nephew. I am telling you Polynices was not just a traitor, fighting for *some* other city. He picked Argos. He picked the other way of life. He picked evil. He picked that which Thebes must at all costs put down if Thebes is to survive, perhaps if Man is to survive, Man as we know him, Man if we are going to be able to respect him.

ANTIGONE: You don't understand. I may not know anything about war but I know something about my brother. He was to be king. Then Creon wouldn't let him be.

TUTOR: He was wholly unfit to be king. To save the city, Creon had to take over . . .

ANTIGONE: I wouldn't doubt it for a moment. Of course Creon had to take over. But can't you imagine that poor boy's feelings? Surely you can't expect *him* to think Creon should take over? Of course not. So he asked himself how he could spite Creon the most, and went over to our worst enemy. That's only human!

TUTOR: Polynices was not human! You don't know what he agreed to . . .

ANTIGONE: What did he . . . agree to?

TUTOR: That I am not authorized to say.

ANTIGONE: There is more? You have not told me all? (*Pause.*) Then I know what I must do.

TUTOR: And what is that?

ANTIGONE: Go straight to Creon. (ANTIGONE *starts to go.*)

  Gong.

II

Council Chamber. CREON *at his desk. To him,* ANTIGONE. *They look at each other.*

ANTIGONE: Thank you for sending the Tutor to talk to me. It helped. It *would* have helped, anyway, if he hadn't got your message all mixed up. Or substituted his own stuffy ideas for yours. He says traitors forfeit the right to be buried and Polynices was a traitor.

CREON: I should have come to you myself. Only the war keeps me busy. (*Smiling.*) This war needs me! (*Pause.*) I evaded being the bearer of bad tidings, I admit it. I was the cause of their badness after all . . . I evaded the issue even in telling the Tutor to soften the blow. Blows like this cannot be softened, can they? It is terrible that you should have to receive them. I deliberately avoided seeing you receive them.

ANTIGONE: I just want to hear you say Polynices wasn't a traitor. Not the way they all mean it. So of course my Uncle Creon will overrule all their stupid prejudices,

16

bring the body of Polynices home to Thebes, and bury it.

CREON: You respect your Uncle Creon, don't you?

ANTIGONE: Respect is something I learned *from* Uncle Creon. Like just about everything else.

CREON: I wanted to hear you say that, because I'm going to ask you to leave all that concerns your brother's death to me. Ask me no further questions. Take on trust that I shall do what's best. Will you?

ANTIGONE (*hesitating*): Well . . .

CREON: Thank you. I'll come tomorrow at the usual hour.

ANTIGONE: There's just one matter . . .

CREON: Well?

ANTIGONE: The arrangements for the burial . . .

CREON: You're leaving them to me.

ANTIGONE: Then, when? Where?

CREON: Be careful, child, how many questions you ask, and how hard you push for the answer. Take your courage in both hands and know: your brother Polynices can't be buried. And for your own sake, do not ask me to explain.

ANTIGONE: Is the truth so ugly? You think I cannot bear to see the body? (*Pause.*) Is it unrecognizable? (*Pause.*) Is there no body left to bury? None that you know is his? I can take even that. Let's pick a body at random from the battle's pile, call it Polynices, and give it its due and our devotions. (*Silence.*) Uncle, what is it?

CREON: You didn't even know your brother.

ANTIGONE: No, not really.

CREON: And if you had, you wouldn't have loved him.

ANTIGONE: I suppose not.

CREON: Thebes' enemies are yours. *My* enemies are yours.

ANTIGONE: That's true. It's only that . . .

CREON: That what?

ANTIGONE: The traitor has been punished. Can't the brother be buried?

CREON: The people say: dead is dead and burial never helped anybody.

ANTIGONE: They also say: a brother is a brother.

CREON: Why does this mean so much to you, my child?

ANTIGONE: Why must a brother be buried? How can you ask? Oh, I don't mean *I* know! Perhaps I don't. But you? Surely you know?

CREON: It's a question of war, of statecraft. Stay away! I have tried to salvage you from the wreckage of your family, tried to spare you the destiny of great ones, so you can just be human, lead a human life, be a woman, be a wife, a mother. What else has it meant, your life with me, our hours together in the colonnade? I am trying to keep you . . . intact.

ANTIGONE: I only want to bury my brother.

CREON: Surely, after the upbringing I've given you, you don't still have your father in you, child, his way of asking questions?

ANTIGONE: Father asked big terrible questions: what I am asking is quite small.

CREON: My reasons for refusing are not small.

ANTIGONE: All the more reason why I should know them.

CREON: Upon your head be it. Antigone, this is a matter of political necessity: it is *necessary* to our city—to the Thebes we all love—that Polynices not be buried.

ANTIGONE: How could it be?

CREON: Thebes has won a battle. It remains to win the war. We estimate: one further blow to their morale will finish them. He'll strike this blow.

ANTIGONE (*amazed*):   How?

CREON: The Argives are religious. They believe that Polynices' soul can't enter Heaven till he is buried. Meanwhile, so they think, their army's under a curse. It follows that that corpse is worth a thousand men to us—provided only it remain unburied. It may even make the difference between defeat and victory.

Pause.

ANTIGONE: But this is outrageous! What had Polynices ever done to you that you should play with him like this? Oh, don't tell me again he was a traitor and that . . .

CREON: The Tutor didn't tell you what Polynices . . . agreed to? (*Pause.*) It has been the custom in this war for both armies to rest one day each week, the first, and on that day the prisoners are exchanged, the wounded carried from the field. Not long ago it occurred to the King of Argos that this was a custom that could be suspended.

ANTIGONE: But Polynices would never . . .

CREON: He had placed Polynices at the head of his army, and he proposed to him, at this point, that, next time, when the Theban army should rest, according to the custom, the Argives should not: they should seek out the Thebans where they slept or drank or tended the wounded and cut them to pieces.

ANTIGONE: That wouldn't be a battle, it would be a massacre!

CREON: It would give anyone pause, wouldn't it? It even gave Polynices pause. And to that pause we owe our lives. And equally: to that pause he owes his death. For in the pause I got the whole story from my spies. Then I waited to hear if Polynices would agree to massacre us. Two days ago I learned that he had so agreed.

ANTIGONE: Oh! So my brother was a monster!

CREON: At last you see it! At last you see how greatly we were provoked! You will concede then that we only did what was necessary. We had *no alternative* . . .

ANTIGONE: To what?

CREON: The date set was next week. Should I have given them this week to prepare?

ANTIGONE: But what *could* you do?

CREON: What day of the week is today?

ANTIGONE: The second.

CREON: You knew there was a battle yesterday. Didn't you ask yourself how there could be a battle on the day of rest?

ANTIGONE (*ignoring the question*): Oh! No! No!

CREON: Well, let's say, to sum it up, the battle was won the way that battles are won, and in it Polynices fell, victim of an Argive stratagem *to which he had consented.* Antigone, this is not a man a girl can intercede for. This was not just a traitor. This was a man who had passed *all* bounds. (*Pause.*) Obviously I have hurt you. But at least now you understand.

ANTIGONE: Understand? Oh yes, I suppose so. I hear a voice. I hear it say things. I think I know what those things are. I *think* I do. But where's my Uncle? I don't hear his voice. Who's speaking?

CREON: Creon.

ANTIGONE: Not my Uncle Creon. He never ordered any massacre. Polynices, yes, he was bad . . . Do you mean that the King of Thebes is as bad a man as the King of Argos?

CREON: The King of Argos is a more original man: the idea of the massacre was all his.

ANTIGONE: But you . . . how could you change from one day to the next? One day the gentle Uncle of the colonnade, next day a . . . Oh, I begin to . . . (ANTIGONE *stops herself from saying "hate you."*) But no, just let me ask yet again: Why, why can I not bury . . .

CREON (*flaring up*): You are not paying attention, little girl! (*Angrily beginning over.*) When Argos threatened to destroy us, what were we to do? Old Tiresias said the stars in their courses were going to fight for us. So? I should have left it to the stars in their courses, should I? My son Haemon said we should fight for Freedom *even if we lose:* Freedom itself would be the winner. Fine consolation! But I knew what had to be done. To stop Argos we had to copy Argos. From a free city we had to make a city of soldiers, police, informers, forced laborers . . . In short, Antigone, what the Tutor told you of Argos is becoming true of Thebes. Perforce. You see how lucky you are to live secluded behind palace walls, among colonnades and fountains? How does one win in war, in politics? By having more power. How does one get more power? In two ways: by violence and by fraud. What follows? That we had to excel Argos in violence and in fraud. Yesterday we did.

Pause.

ANTIGONE: The massacre. You did order it . . .

CREON: What alternative did I have? You have named none. Besides, child, you know nothing of the whole chain of events in which this . . . massacre is but one link. A massacre is an abstract thing, anyway. I could tell you things that hurt far more. Having to remove Tiresias from my path, for instance: I revered that old man. And removing Haemon from my path—my only son. Driving him into the mountains where he would become the leader of all those who hate Creon. What is a massacre to that?

ANTIGONE (*ignoring what* CREON *is saying*): You ordered the massacre.

CREON: Say, rather: you have been shown today the gangrene in the bones of the world. (*Pause.*) Think all this over, my child. I don't expect you to absorb it all at once. But at least you know now why your brother will not, cannot, be buried.

ANTIGONE (*brokenly*): Oh yes. Yes. At least I know that, don't I? And now your war "needs you," doesn't it? I'm sorry I took all this time from your war. (*Unsteadily,* ANTIGONE *leaves.*)

Gong.

FIRST SLAVE: As Antigone made her way back slowly to the palace, she seemed to be holding her breath.

SECOND SLAVE: Suddenly when she arrived at the colonnade the words came.

ANTIGONE: I know what I will do: I will bury Polynices myself. Right now! Go out, and do it! That'll give Creon something to think about! (*Pause.*) My feet don't move. Why is my mind so full of Creon's words warning, threatening me? "Polynices' body is worth"—how many hundred men was it? Bury it and Argos fights with strength renewed! So much the worse for Thebes. It wasn't smart of Creon to leave me free! (*Starts out again. Stops.*) Would I hurt Thebes? And cause the death of Thebans? Polynices must be buried. But why? I don't really know. Who could help me? If *I* can't do it, then who could?

FIRST SLAVE: That night Antigone tossed on a sleepless bed.

SECOND SLAVE: But before dawn she woke with Creon's words ringing in her ears.

FIRST SLAVE: "Removing Haemon from my path. Driving him into the mountains."

SECOND SLAVE: Rising early, she hurried to the city gate.

FIRST SLAVE: Creon's guards let her pass. And she strode on toward the mountains.

SECOND SLAVE: Seven hours later a sentry brought her to Haemon's tent.

III

Haemon's tent. HAEMON. *To him,* ANTIGONE.

HAEMON: So it's true. "A girl who says she's Princess Antigone." That's how my sentry put it. "A young woman,"
they should have said, hm? Let me look at you, "Princess Antigone." (*Pause. He looks at her.*) So you found
your way up here all by yourself? What for?

ANTIGONE: I need help.

HAEMON: I see. Well, I suppose we can leave this till tomorrow? You must be worn out.

ANTIGONE: I can't wait till tomorrow.

HAEMON: Suppose the Commander-in-Chief can't see you today? Not cousin Haemon but the Commander-in-Chief.
Of the Liberation Forces. Unless your business is with
the Commander, and not with the cousin?

ANTIGONE: It is. I want to know if what Creon says is true.
He says he . . . ordered a massacre. Yesterday.

HAEMON: My dear, you don't need me to tell you that. It is
history now.

ANTIGONE: But Creon . . . does order massacres?

HAEMON: He ordered this one.

ANTIGONE: Then you know why I am here.

HAEMON: You have broken with him. I should have known. Should have known you would, you must. How old are you now, Antigone? Sixteen? (ANTIGONE *nods*.) It's early . . . to learn the score. Did it hurt very much?

ANTIGONE: I don't propose to spend my life feeling sorry for myself.

HAEMON: That's my girl. You *were* to be mine, weren't you? Maybe you *will* be mine, even. In another sense.

ANTIGONE: I feel that. That brought me here. But what do I know of you? Or your "Liberation Forces"? Oh, I saw your sentries and your tents. But how is a bunch of boys camping out in the mountains ever going to make headway against Creon?

HAEMON: Good question. Of course, I might just turn it around and ask how any little king of a single city is going to make headway against the younger generation of all Greece? But I won't quibble with you. You want to know our master strategy, don't you?

ANTIGONE: I suppose that's what it's called.

HAEMON: You've earned the right to. Having come over to our side, you've earned the right to know what we are all about. As my cousin, you shall even know our secret hopes.

ANTIGONE: Yes?

HAEMON: At the right moment we shall start an insurrection in the city, sweep down with reinforcements from these mountains, depose Creon, liberate Thebes. And, with luck, induce the youth of other cities to do the same.

ANTIGONE: But how can you possibly defeat Creon if even Argos hasn't been able to, in three years of war?

HAEMON: You are a strategist already. That is one of two key questions. What would the other one be?

ANTIGONE (*slowly*): What to do about Argos?

HAEMON: Exactly. Not much use taking Thebes if then we are confronted with the armies of Argos. Or, alternatively, suppose Argos defeats Thebes. How, as you would put it, can we "possibly defeat" an Argos which at that point is Argos and Thebes combined? "How can we possibly?" Or are we tangling with *im*possibilities? As Creon thinks. As Argos thinks. But as you evidently don't think; or you wouldn't be here.

ANTIGONE (*simply*): I had nowhere else to go.

HAEMON (*laughs*): Well, maybe you have confidence in my judgment. At any rate you come at a good time. One of those bad times which is a good time. Yesterday at this hour I wouldn't have known what to tell you. For some months despair had been spreading here like the mountain mists. Some of our people had drifted away. Maybe all of them would have. But now, as you say: the massacre.

ANTIGONE: It helps *you*?

HAEMON: You're shocked, and so you should be. We order no massacres. We are against Creon because *he* orders them. He copies Argos. We don't. And yet, this massacre may prove useful to us.

ANTIGONE: How can that be?

HAEMON: Antigone, did Creon tell you about your brother?

ANTIGONE: Oh yes, that's why . . .

HAEMON: I can imagine how you feel about that. Well, so do we. Only more so. Or differently so. For us it is a concrete issue. Of political, of historic importance. You know Creon's calculation?

ANTIGONE: The Argives are religious. They believe Polynices' body can't enter the next world until he is buried, and until that time their army is under a curse.

HAEMON: Unburied, the body of Polynices is worth a lot to Creon. *Therefore,* buried, it is worth a lot to . . .

ANTIGONE: Argos.

HAEMON: I was going to say: to us.

ANTIGONE: So you want Polynices buried? Why?

HAEMON: Victory hangs in the balance. Yesterday's massacre has weighted the scale very heavily on the side of Thebes. Not burying Polynices puts more weight on the same side of the scale. Creon even hopes for *final* victory from this ploy.

ANTIGONE (*slowly*): As things are, Argos can scarcely win.

HAEMON: Argos can scarcely win. Argos can *almost* win. And what is it to almost win? It is to almost lose. And so it is to have the other side almost win, too. Creon's massacre weighted the scale on the Theban side. Should Polynices be buried, that would weigh the scale on the Argive side. When a scale is weighed equally on both sides, Antigone, what is the result?

ANTIGONE: Equilibrium?

HAEMON: Two giants of equal weight and equal fighting skill engaged in mortal combat—a very special kind of equilibrium, hm? When they are through fighting, there will be nothing of theirs left. So the little folk can come creeping out of their holes—and live!

ANTIGONE (*pause*): And to this, the burial of Polynices would be a . . . great contribution? (*Pause.*) Oh, Haemon, sometimes one feels that all things work together for good! Do you know why I came here? No, not exactly because I'd broken with Creon. I came here to ask you to bury Polynices! And now I find that's just what you're going to do! (*Pause.*) Isn't it?

HAEMON: It would be. If I could find a way. Antigone, we would already have buried your brother but we can't get at the body. Between these mountains and Polynices stands Creon's army.

ANTIGONE: Don't you have people in Thebes who could do it?

HAEMON: Who *would* do it, yes. But they can't get out of Thebes. Creon's guards take care of that.

ANTIGONE: I got out of Thebes. Creon has left me free. No doubt because he doesn't think me capable of doing anything.

HAEMON: And you would be free again? If you returned, you could leave—for the battlefield where your brother's body is?

ANTIGONE: As far as I know.

Pause.

HAEMON: The burial of Polynices would be a great contribution, Antigone.

Pause.

ANTIGONE (*in a low voice*): You are asking *me* to do it?

HAEMON: I can hardly do that. You are hardly even ours as yet. And this is a man's job. The culprit can expect to be punished. Even you would be. Clapped in jail, who knows for how long?

ANTIGONE: I *should* do it, I know. I have known that from the start. But when I tried to set out for the battlefield, my feet just wouldn't move. I am only here, asking you to do this, Haemon, because I found I *couldn't* do it myself.

HAEMON: Why *was* that?

ANTIGONE: Why *was* that? Oh, Haemon, the answer is so simple you won't see it! *I am a coward.* That's why!

HAEMON: That is *too* simple. In the beginning, you doubtless didn't have the conviction, the passion . . .

ANTIGONE: Nonsense! I was carried away with passion, the greatest passion of them all: hate! Hatred for Creon! I could have scratched his eyes out or taken a knife to him! (*Suddenly stops.*) And yet when I tried to walk toward the city gate I was *scared.*

HAEMON: Then you came to the man who would hate Creon even more?

ANTIGONE: His son, yes, whom, as he told me, he had destroyed!

HAEMON: Well, now we can nail down your first mistake, Antigone: hatred is not what steels men for great deeds. Of course you stopped in your tracks! I don't hate my father: I object to him. This movement I lead is not a hate movement. The hate movements only burn the house down: we aim to be housekeepers. Oh, Antigone, the Creons come and go. What advances is the Cause, our Cause, the Cause of Freedom. You needn't take my word for that. It is something you will learn—in the service of Freedom. But understand at the outset: it's not a man we're making war on, it is a system. We are not rebellious children, kicking up our heels against our parents. We represent the revolt of all who are young *in spirit* against the old in spirit, against a senile, sick, putrescent Greece. Strictly speaking, we are not rebels at all: we are revolutionaries. Do you know the difference? We shall teach it to you.

ANTIGONE (*trembling*): Why are you talking this way? I mean: if you are not asking me to bury Polynices.

HAEMON: To tell somebody to go out and take the risks while I stay home on my big behind, that goes against the grain with me, little one. What wouldn't I give for the chance to do this deed myself, what a privilege it would be . . .

ANTIGONE: What's a privilege for one is a privilege for another. You *are* asking me to bury Polynices.

HAEMON: I suppose I am. It must seem cruel, presumptuous, even opportunistic.

ANTIGONE: Not at all. It is a very great compliment. That a practical man like you thinks I *can* do it. Why *do* you think so?

HAEMON: Because I know you—from way back. Because I know, too, your . . . place in the scheme of things.

ANTIGONE: What?

HAEMON: You were born to greatness. You were born for greatness. There were prophecies to that effect. Omens. Well, we don't believe in prophecies and omens, do we? Let's speak then of historic destiny. It was your father who defied the Sphinx, repudiated the Olympians. The tyranny of gods was at an end. It remained to end the tyranny of men.

ANTIGONE: I have been brought up to believe I would be spared the fate of great ones.

HAEMON: Well might Creon feed you that stuff! He had himself betrayed the Cause. But that is just the challenge. To us. The son of Creon. The daughter of Oedipus. What Creon has lost, we shall regain. I shall lead our armies into Thebes. You . . . you will recall that I was not surprised to see you? You were the long awaited guest. And yet I did not know—you recall this too?—just why you came: to ask that I bury Polynices. History may not be woven by gods, Antigone, but it is beautifully woven, all the same. You were sent here to find your historic destiny. You will leave here to fulfill it.

ANTIGONE: Can I believe that?

HAEMON: Look into your heart.

ANTIGONE: Oh, Haemon, let me make a confession to you. When Creon told me I was to be normal and happy, it used to make me feel abnormal and unhappy!

HAEMON: Do you know what my image of you has always been? Once I actually drew you with chalk. On horseback. In your upraised hand, a gleaming sword. At your back, your army. Facing you, Creon and his army. I wrote speeches for both of you. Creon: "Rebel against the state, against your king, submit! Down on your knees, and send this mob of schoolboys back to their homes!" Antigone, throwing out her chest, and laughing: "Give me liberty or give me death!"

ANTIGONE (*pause*): Very well then. I will do it.

HAEMON: And you can?

ANTIGONE: Yes. Now I can.

HAEMON: There is no time to be lost. Go! I speak now as your Commander-in-Chief. I, who was expected to love you and marry you, shall do better: I shall revere you —and envy you.

ANTIGONE: I am so calm now. So calm.

HAEMON (*taking her hands*): We shall not let you fall. We shall liberate Thebes. And we shall liberate you. So no farewells, little Antigone. We shall meet again. Go!

ANTIGONE *goes.*

Gong.

FIRST SLAVE: And she descended from the mountains and returned to Thebes.

SECOND SLAVE: Next day she set out for the battlefield.

FIRST SLAVE: The battlefield had woods on either side. The body of Polynices had been placed on a mound in a clearing. A soldier stood guard.

Gong.

IV

A clearing. The body of Polynices in the background. SOLDIER *on guard. Silence. Then, a sound.*

SOLDIER: Who's that? Give the password!

Enter an OFFICER.

OFFICER: "Creon." "Creon" is the password. I should know, shouldn't I?

SOLDIER: Sorry, sir. Couldn't see you till now, sir. Never did see you close up. But, yes, I've seen you. At parades. On special occasions. You are Creon's personal adjutant.

OFFICER: Correct. I choose the passwords. And this one is my favorite. Because Thebes is Creon, and Creon is Thebes. Soldier, I am here to stay. Creon wishes me to keep an eye on the Polynices operation until further orders.

SOLDIER: Welcome to our graveyard, sir.

OFFICER: Good joke! Ha, ha! But don't distract me. I bear a message from your king.

SOLDIER: Yes, sir?

OFFICER: His niece, Princess Antigone, has taken it into her head to come here. May arrive any minute.

SOLDIER: Yes, sir.

OFFICER: That's the message. You already have your orders. (*Pause.*) Don't you?

SOLDIER: Yes, sir.

OFFICER: Good, then. We can leave it at that?

SOLDIER (*tentatively*): You mean His Majesty wants an exception made—for members of the family like?

OFFICER (*thrown*): What?!

SOLDIER: The penalty for attempting to bury that body there is death. Right?

OFFICER: Right.

SOLDIER: What's the Princess coming out here for anyway? To see the sunset?

OFFICER: Don't be impertinent.

SOLDIER: Sorry, sir.

OFFICER: She may try to bury her brother. Yes.

SOLDIER: So where does that leave me?

OFFICER: A soldier carries out orders, doesn't he? He does that. He does nothing but that. He exists for no other reason but that. Hm?

SOLDIER: Sure. As far as soldiering goes. And I'm reliable. Or they wouldn't have picked me for this particular job, right?

OFFICER: Right.

SOLDIER: But this isn't a battle. One girl isn't the enemy army. And a girl that's our king's niece isn't an enemy girl.

OFFICER (*ponderously*): But your king is still your king. And he's gone to the trouble of sending a special messenger to explain that, even in the circumstances you describe, orders are still orders.

SOLDIER: So I gotta kill a princess, huh?

OFFICER: Nothing of the sort! Antigone doesn't yet know what the penalty is! Telling her will be quite enough.

SOLDIER: Not if she's anything like the rest of her family.

OFFICER: What on earth do you mean, soldier?

SOLDIER: Oh, you know. Always looking for nets to get tangled up in or pins to put their eyes out with.

OFFICER: Antigone won't.

SOLDIER: Let's hope not.

OFFICER: Creon says she won't. And Creon has the knack of being right. He has been right every time. And he *will* be right every time. Creon has informed me that when Antigone is told the penalty—by you—she will turn round and go home.

SOLDIER: And in case our ever right king should be wrong for the first time in his life? I mean: just to be ready for every contingency, like the book says.

OFFICER: I will stay till the incident is closed. But not right on the spot. I can't stand the sight of blood. I'm willing to give the orders for blood to be shed, but never, like those barbaric Argive commanders, would I go out and gloat over it! In the unlikely event that you do have to shed blood now, soldier, do you know what I shall do?

SOLDIER: No, sir.

OFFICER: Walk a little further away and look in the other direction.

SOLDIER: We all like to have an out, don't we?

OFFICER: What's that?

SOLDIER: Mine's that I act under orders. If not military orders, then Creon's own kingly orders. Orders. Everyone gets them from someone else. Except Creon. And maybe *he* hears voices. Your "out" is that you're sensitive. You'd never *do* the things you *get* done. No offense, of course. These things gotta be done, just like these orders gotta be obeyed. Right?

OFFICER (*pompously*): But my dear man, there's a principle involved here. Creon banished his own son rather than sacrifice the interests of Thebes to those of family. (*He begins to speechify.*) Shall Creon now refuse to sacrifice . . .

SOLDIER: Someone coming, sir.

OFFICER: What? Oh. Yes. Yes. I'll be over here. (*He walks a few steps away.*)

ANTIGONE *enters.*

SOLDIER: The password.

ANTIGONE: What?

SOLDIER: Where are you going, anyway?

ANTIGONE: I . . . I have business here.

SOLDIER: You have business here? What do *I* have?

ANTIGONE: I don't know.

SOLDIER: Being here *is* my business. Like to swap jobs with me? I'd like to swap apartments with *you.*

ANTIGONE (*startled*): You know me?

SOLDIER: Doesn't everybody?

ANTIGONE: Then, if you know me, let me pass, I beg you! (*Pause.*) I order you!

SOLDIER: You order me! And you didn't even know the password. The password is "Creon." Say it. Come on, say it. All right, I'll say it: "Creon"! But then I must add that Creon—same man as the password—says no one can pass anyway.

ANTIGONE: I just want to see my brother's body. Give me five minutes. After all, you could have been gone for five minutes. And I'll pay the penalty.

SOLDIER: What? Pay the penalty? Really?

ANTIGONE: Certainly. I'm not afraid.

SOLDIER: Do you know what the penalty *is?!*

ANTIGONE: Oh, Creon can lock me up. I'm ready for that!

SOLDIER: Then you *don't* know what it is.

ANTIGONE: I hate him so much I don't care anymore *what* he does to me. I can face it!

SOLDIER (*after a teasing pause*): Well, miss, then I have the painful duty of informing you that the punishment is death.

ANTIGONE: Imprisonment till death?!

SOLDIER: Death without imprisonment. *Here.* With this spear and this knife. Followed by burning with pomp and ceremony. *There.* So everyone sees you.

ANTIGONE: Strike me down where I stand? You couldn't!

SOLDIER: Oh?

ANTIGONE: You're a Theban, aren't you? Didn't your mother bring you up on Theban principles? Didn't she tell you Man's fate is Man?

SOLDIER: Come to think of it, she never did.

ANTIGONE: What about Theban Freedom? Don't you love Freedom?

SOLDIER: What?

ANTIGONE (*bitterly*): Then what *do* you love? Money? I have that, too.

SOLDIER: Madam, we are in the presence of King Creon's personal adjutant.

OFFICER (*coming forward*): That will be enough, my man. Princess, I apologize for the tone this fellow took with you, it's an affront to all the traditions of the Theban Army. But what he says is true.

ANTIGONE: Are *you* bribable? Oh, don't take offense. I have plenty of money and it's all yours! My brother must be buried at any cost!

OFFICER: Offense or no offense, that will not be possible, Princess.

ANTIGONE *looks from one to the other. The* SOLDIER *wears a half-amused smile. The* OFFICER *is correct.*

ANTIGONE: "Give me liberty or give me death!" (*Suddenly, piercingly.*) Oh, how I hate you, Creon, hate you, hate you, hate you! (*Neither man changes his demeanor.* ANTIGONE *turns and goes.*)

OFFICER: "When she is told the penalty, she will turn around and go home." Creon is always right, my man.

Gong.

FIRST SLAVE: And Antigone walked back to the city gate and through the narrow streets of Thebes to her wing of the palace.

SECOND SLAVE: She sat on her bed.

ANTIGONE: Creon wins. And how simply! No wonder he left me free to leave the city, free even to bury Polynices— at the cost of my life. Who would give his life for such a thing as this, a formality . . .? But then it isn't, is it? No, no, no, Polynices must be buried, I may not know anything else but I know that. So someone must pay the price. Who? (*Pause.*) I don't want to die! I'm too young! And I don't believe in Freedom. I only thought I did. If I'd believed, then, when I had my chance to bury Polynices, wouldn't I have buried him? And then: been buried myself? At sixteen? Without ever becoming the woman, wife, and mother I was meant for? Meant for! I disgust myself. I am meant for *nothing*.

FIRST SLAVE: And she threw open the window, climbed up on the sill, crawled outside, and prepared to leap to her death.

SECOND SLAVE: But, looking down, she broke out in a sweat, and staggered back.

FIRST SLAVE: She fell fainting on the bed. This time, although it was broad day, she was soon asleep.

SECOND SLAVE: And again the voice of Creon rang in her ears.

FIRST SLAVE: This time it spoke of Tiresias whom, with Haemon, he had removed from state affairs.

SECOND SLAVE: When Antigone awoke, though it was past midnight, she got up, left the palace, and made her way to the hut where Tiresias lived in the shadow of the city wall.

Gong.

V

Tiresias' hut. TIRESIAS. *To him,* ANTIGONE.

TIRESIAS: Antigone? Here? Now?

ANTIGONE: You recognize me? I thought you were blind.

TIRESIAS: Tush, child. My boy saw you coming. Have you come to me for sympathy?

ANTIGONE: Yes. I have no one else to turn to.

TIRESIAS: Tiresias cannot condone cowardice.

ANTIGONE: You know all, then?

TIRESIAS: Creon has massacred the Argives. Your brother was one of the victims. You went out to bury him. You did not do it.

ANTIGONE: You do know all. Do you know what the penalty is?

TIRESIAS: The penalty is death. Naturally. Gloriously. Such was your opportunity. Such, surely, is your mission as the daughter of Oedipus.

ANTIGONE: My . . . mission?

TIRESIAS: Oh come, don't trifle with me.

ANTIGONE: I'm *not* trifling with you. But don't you realize Creon brought me up to be a wife and mother? That was *his* idea of my mission.

TIRESIAS: Whose daughter are you? Do you mean to tell me that, whatever Creon and his creatures might say, your *heart* never said anything? Did your heart not tell you you were destined for greatness? Did not a voice whisper that you had a glorious mission?

ANTIGONE: Sometimes it did, but why should I believe such voices? A voice spoke yesterday that I had to believe. It said, "You cannot die for Freedom."

TIRESIAS: Freedom?

ANTIGONE: Oh, then you don't know of my trip to the mountains?

TIRESIAS: Ah, so. You also went to see your cousin Haemon?

ANTIGONE: Of course, isn't this what interests my generation —revolution? We are going to liberate Thebes!

TIRESIAS: Yes? And burying Polynices was to help?

ANTIGONE: Very much so. It was to help the Argives . . . who would knock out the Thebans . . . who would knock out the Argives. *We* would then come out of our holes and live.

TIRESIAS: So why *didn't* you bury Polynices?

ANTIGONE: I don't want to die.

TIRESIAS: Oh?

ANTIGONE: Even Haemon didn't foresee that would be the penalty. (*Defensively.*) There was never any question of my dying.

TIRESIAS: So that is that, then.

ANTIGONE: Yes. That is that.

TIRESIAS: And you came to me . . . because you had no one else to turn to.

ANTIGONE: I had tried Haemon.

TIRESIAS: The two great Creon-haters—you sought them both out?

ANTIGONE: Only Haemon doesn't hate Creon.

TIRESIAS: Nor do I.

Pause.

ANTIGONE: I'm not sure I follow this conversation, but I realize when I'm not welcome. Goodbye, Tiresias.

Silence.

TIRESIAS: You haven't left. *Why* haven't you left? Why are you here in the first place?

ANTIGONE: I told you. Because at least you won't preach Freedom at me!

TIRESIAS: Oh, that isn't what you said. It's better. It's what you should have said. Because I won't preach Freedom at you. And, if not Freedom, what was it you expected me to preach?

ANTIGONE: *You* tell *me*. Preach it even, if you feel like it.

TIRESIAS: Come in girl.

ANTIGONE *is still in the doorway.*

And sit down.

She squats on the floor.

I owe you an apology. I thought you'd tried something and failed. You had tried something else, though. Something which is *foredoomed* to failure.

ANTIGONE: What is that?

TIRESIAS: Freedom is a phantom. No wonder you couldn't die for it! And it would have been a pitiful waste.

ANTIGONE: Why *should* Polynices be buried?

TIRESIAS: Aye, there's the question! Let me ask you another. Antigone, would you call yourself an atheist?

ANTIGONE: I wasn't reared to believe in Zeus, Apollo, and the rest, if that's what you mean.

TIRESIAS: Do you believe in a Higher Law than that of the State?

ANTIGONE: I *feel* . . . there must be . . . something of the sort . . .

TIRESIAS: The rites of death are sacred. The State has the right to kill a traitor, not to maltreat his body. Do you see that?

ANTIGONE: Yes, yes . . . I see . . . I see . . .

TIRESIAS: That is the Unwritten Law. Transcending written laws. It is divine. It is of God. Such is my "preachment," anyhow. Are you receptive to it?

ANTIGONE: Maybe I am. Yes, I think I am.

TIRESIAS: What brought you to me?

ANTIGONE: You keep asking that!

TIRESIAS: When we know the answer we shall know all we need to know.

ANTIGONE: Well, after I tried to kill myself, I went to sleep and . . .

TIRESIAS: You tried to kill yourself?!

ANTIGONE: Sort of. Yes.

TIRESIAS: That's important. How?

ANTIGONE: I was going to jump out of the window. I mean I thought I was.

TIRESIAS: You left the prince unburied because you couldn't bear to be killed. Then you proposed to be killed— but without burying the prince.

ANTIGONE: The guard's knife scared me!

TIRESIAS: So you proceeded to contemplate a yet more painful death.

ANTIGONE: That scared me too!

TIRESIAS: And thus you passed from one mock death to the other. *Then* what did you do?

ANTIGONE: Came here.

TIRESIAS: Ah! At last we have the whole sequence!

ANTIGONE: Sequence?

TIRESIAS: Three deaths. One more real than the next. The third one . . .

ANTIGONE: What?!

TIRESIAS: Completely real. Gloriously real.

ANTIGONE: You like the word "glorious," don't you?

TIRESIAS: Yes. When it fits.

ANTIGONE: You are a funny man. First you despise me and try to get me out of the house. Next you want to kill me—"gloriously." (*Pause.*) Have you no qualms about asking a young girl to go out and die for *your* ideals?

TIRESIAS: Have we established the main point, then?

ANTIGONE: How d'you mean?

TIRESIAS: That you *could* die for the ideals you call "mine"? You could not die for Haemon's ideals: that was proved. The ideals you could die for are . . . otherwise. But they exist. Yes?

ANTIGONE: You are a hard man to fight.

TIRESIAS: You came here for a fight? I thought you came here to *avoid* a fight—with Creon's guards? Not to mention your fight with yourself?

ANTIGONE: Tiresias, what are you trying to get me to do?

TIRESIAS: Would you say that again?

Pause.

ANTIGONE: You always *were* a prophet, weren't you?

TIRESIAS: I always was a prophet of a certain kind.

ANTIGONE: What kind was that?

TIRESIAS: I made my entrance in the penultimate scene of the tragedy—to announce the ultimate scene.

ANTIGONE: And now you are eager to . . . make one of your entrances?

TIRESIAS: Who was it made an entrance in *this* scene? You came here. Why did you?

ANTIGONE: Again!

TIRESIAS: Again.

Long pause.

ANTIGONE: To find the courage to bury Polynices.

TIRESIAS: To find the courage to die.

ANTIGONE: Yes. But I am a fumbler, Tiresias. I went first to Haemon . . .

TIRESIAS: And in this way God's pattern reveals itself. That you tried unsuccessfully to believe in Freedom was no misfortune but a blessing, for without it you could not have reached despair. And your despair was no misfortune but a blessing for without it you could not have learned to will your own death. To take your own life is a sin, and yet your wish to take it was a blessing, for from that wish came this wish: to go to Tiresias' hut.

ANTIGONE: And learn to die.

TIRESIAS: For whose ideals?

ANTIGONE: God's. The true ones. Mine—they're becoming mine, aren't they?

TIRESIAS: They always were. Who is killing you?

ANTIGONE: No one is killing me.

TIRESIAS: Correct. How gladly would I myself not die in this Cause! But what good would that do, even if they would let me? I am not chosen. When my boy told me he saw you coming I was on my knees praying for a deliverer. "The blood of Polynices cries out from the ground: Woe to Creon, maker of massacres!" You are the answer to my prayer.

ANTIGONE: When death is glorious, who could not die?

TIRESIAS: And in this way both Thebes and Argos are prevented from plunging Greece into total darkness.

ANTIGONE: I wish I didn't go on hating Creon. Haemon told me not to. But then I did!

TIRESIAS: And did not bury Polynices! We owe Creon's laws obedience and respect except when they infringe the Higher Law.

ANTIGONE: But now they do!

TIRESIAS: And now they do. And you will disobey, not in hate, but in the name of God. Will you pray with me, Antigone?

ANTIGONE: Yes.

TIRESIAS: Let us pray in silence to our God!

They kneel.

ANTIGONE (*still on her knees*): Oh, Tiresias, when Haemon told me how he had always seen Antigone, I saw her too. And now as we pray to "God" I see her again. In my mind's eye, is it, or is she really there?

TIRESIAS: She is really there. I see the chosen one; though the mind's eye is the only eye I've got.

ANTIGONE: She's really there. Yes, there! Look at the splendid charger, white all over. Look at the gleaming sword in my upraised hand! There are my men, in the rear. And there, in front, is Creon with his host. It's the same as

Haemon said. The same but better, somehow. Listen. Creon is vowing defiance. Now comes my answer. What? That's not what I said before! What am I saying?

TIRESIAS (*rising*): Yes, what are you saying?

ANTIGONE (*rising*): "I am the King's loyal subject but God's first!"

TIRESIAS: At last you have found the strength. Farewell. It will be enough to take a handful of earth and sprinkle the body.

Gong.

VI

The clearing. SOLDIER. OFFICER *enters, running.*

OFFICER: Someone is visible from the hilltop. Stand ready.

SOLDIER: Huh? Who is it this time?

OFFICER: We couldn't tell. But you'll see them well before they arrive. From that direction. Stand on the mound. (SOLDIER *does so.*) What do you see?

SOLDIER: A cloud of dust. My God, it's that princess again.

OFFICER: Antigone, again? (*Pause. He verifies the report.*) This is something Creon did not bargain for.

SOLDIER: Hey, wait a minute. The dust's dying down. There's someone else with her!

OFFICER (*races onto the mound*): What? (*He shields his eyes to look.*) Great heavens, you're right. A man. But he's not with her. Watch. He's overtaking her. He's overtaken her. No word passed between them. (*Pause.*) He limps. I should know that limp. See the big head? The jutting ears? You know who that is? Assface we all called him.

The slave of Polynices before he left Thebes. Got left behind. But loved his master. He was probably the only man who ever did. It's obvious what *he* intends to do.

SOLDIER: Bury Polynices?

OFFICER: Exactly.

SOLDIER: Think he knows the penalty?

OFFICER: With him, knowing the penalty will make no difference.

SOLDIER: With *her,* knowing the penalty has made no difference. (*Silence.*) You know what to do, of course, don't you, sir?

OFFICER: Creon said: when she knew the penalty was death, she'd see reason. That's what death's for, he added, so men will see reason.

SOLDIER: Don't say Creon can be wrong?

OFFICER: Wait a minute. If death makes men see reason . . . If she knew the penalty was death. If she knew this *death,* which is the penalty . . . Soldier, Creon was right, but his rightness is like that of the Fates, it bides its time. Antigone will see reason. And the Fates have sent Assface to make her see it.

SOLDIER: Huh?

OFFICER: Kill Assface. According to your orders. As soon as he arrives. And here. Carry his body to that pyre and burn it.

SOLDIER: Kill an idiot? Without giving him the option of toddling off home?

OFFICER: Are you reliable or are you not?

Pause.

SOLDIER: I'm reliable.

OFFICER: Good. Men do not die for nothing in Creon's Thebes. Antigone will see the whole thing. She has never seen death: this too Creon pointed out. She will see it now. She will know what it is, this penalty. And she will see reason.

Gong.

FIRST SLAVE: Assface seemed not to hear the warning. Well knowing what would follow, the officer turned away so as not to see the blood. The soldier drew his long knife, stood right in the path of Assface, holding the knife straight out in front. Assface sidestepped it.

SECOND SLAVE: Assface was within three feet of the body when the soldier caught up with him. The knife entered his back. Assface stopped as if someone had clapped him upon the shoulder. The knife had gone right through him but he did not see it, still had not seen it when the soldier withdrew it with a jerk. Assface rolled now, gently, like a ship; then, fell on his face.

FIRST SLAVE: Still on his face, he dragged himself the few remaining inches to Polynices, propped himself on his arms, and said: "Master! Master!"

SECOND SLAVE: Then with a smile he died.

FIRST SLAVE: The officer returned in time to help the soldier throw Assface on the pyre.

SECOND SLAVE: And thus the body of Polynices was unguarded and Antigone got her second chance.

FIRST SLAVE: She did not take it but said: "Was that death?" and vomited.

SECOND SLAVE: A second time Antigone retraced her steps to the city gate and thence to her own wing of the palace.

FIRST SLAVE: She had "seen reason" and all night and all day was in high fever.

SECOND SLAVE: But when Creon came to see her in the evening, the fever was gone.

Gong.

VII

Antigone's wing of the palace. ANTIGONE. To her, CREON.

ANTIGONE: I am better.
CREON: That's good news, my child.
ANTIGONE: I intended to bury Polynices.
CREON: My guards reported that.
ANTIGONE: I went to see Haemon.
CREON: Yes.
ANTIGONE: And Tiresias.
CREON: Yes, yes.
ANTIGONE: I thought they'd arm my spirit. (*Pause.*) They
    would have, too. But my spirit is no good. Heroic sacrifice
    is good in dreams of youths in rebel bands on fire with
    Freedom or girls with shining faces and outstretched
    arms, but when you see death, even a happy death, prob-
    ably painless, like that of Assface, see the limbs crumple
    and the breathing stop, Freedom, God, *all* the words
    come tumbling down. You may believe things but you

don't believe them *that* much. So: I shall not bury Polynices, and Polynices will not be buried.

CREON: I had not thought the shock would be as great as this.

ANTIGONE: Which shock? Discovering "the gangrene in the bones of the world"?

CREON: There was another?

ANTIGONE: Discovering the gangrene in the bones of Creon. (*Pause.*) I shouldn't have said that. You're no worse than anyone else. But, oh, my Uncle Creon was so much better than anyone else! It's a shock to find he's not there. The man who's there wouldn't know why a girl might want to bury her own brother. He has no feelings.

CREON: And *that* is what all this has meant to you? That Creon is inhuman? Could feel nothing for Polynices? Imagine nothing of what you felt?

ANTIGONE: That's all.

CREON: Then my dear child, you have learned less than nothing: you have learned what is not so. I am haunted by a thought, a hallucination almost, that comes to me at night, by day, in sleep, in idle moments, or when I'm at work. *I see myself stealing out in the dead of night through the city gate on to the battlefield and there— burying Polynices.*

ANTIGONE: You see . . . ?

CREON: You say I wouldn't know why a girl would want to bury her own brother. You think I don't care. Tell me then: why *does* a girl wish to bury her own brother?

ANTIGONE (*bitterly*): Why indeed? Had I but known, my recent history would have been different. Was it for form's sake? Or because everybody's doing it? I heard what Haemon had to say and old Tiresias. You have been silent.

CREON: If I broke silence now, would you admit I know your heart?

ANTIGONE: I'm listening.

CREON: I understand what you have said of Haemon and Tiresias. They are public men like me, and have their public reasons. Yours are private ones. And so in this affair of Polynices you told me right off: I could kill the traitor, you wished to bury the brother. That was all: no dreams of Liberty or God! To you, all's feeling. Even the State. The State feels like a dragon which, if given a chance, will wrap you in its coils and stifle you. What did you want? To call your soul your own. You wished to keep some part of yourself, and that the center, secure, inviolate, even at the cost of deadly battle with the dragon, wherever you might find him, even coiled round a corpse: the corpse might be your brother's. Your brother was a bad man, men might tell you. His burial will lose Thebes the war, cost innumerable lives, your own included—all this men could tell you but you would not be listening, you would be telling yourself: a corpse is more than a corpse and a brother is always a brother and this body, this brother, is sacred and may not become a counter in a calculation: you were doing what you must do. (*Pause.*) Am I right? Is that why you wished to bury Polynices?

ANTIGONE (*in a low voice*):   Not the part about the innumerable lives: I would not hurt Thebes. But the rest is right. Much righter than Haemon or Tiresias. Why is your voice so vibrant suddenly? You say *I* feel. It seems to me *you* feel . . . (*Stops suddenly.*) Are you telling me you— *you* want Polynices buried?

CREON (*very agitated*):   How should I not? What do you take me for, a hypocrite? A human being should be treated humanly. A man that dies should be given decent burial . . .

ANTIGONE (*quickly*):   Even though it means defeat for Thebes?

CREON (*carried away*):   Yes, but does it? Is that really sure? One doesn't really know these things, Antigone! One consults the experts but d'you know what they do? They disagree! That's all they ever do! At present they're telling me I'm right, but what would you expect? I pay them. One knows nothing, and is haunted by the thought that all these measures which one knew were crimes were also grave miscalculations . . . (*Loudly.*) For a purpose one commits a crime. That purpose not achieved, a larger crime. Still no result? A larger crime still. A larger and a larger . . . (*Pause. Quietly.*) Don't think I've never thought of getting out.

ANTIGONE: *You? You* have thought of killing yourself? Oh! Oh, I begin to see how it is! (*Suddenly.*) *You want me to bury Polynices.*

CREON: What?

ANTIGONE: You want *me* to bury Polynices.

CREON: Is that what you conceive I have been saying?

ANTIGONE (*simply*): You have made it very, very clear.

CREON: Don't fence with me, girl. I only tried to show that wishes like that are known even to Creon.

ANTIGONE: You succeeded.

CREON: *Part of me* wants him buried. Not the wiser part, however. It seems that when you learn that Uncle Creon's feelings run one way while King Creon's reason runs the other, you take for granted it's the king that's wrong. If yesterday you thought I'd killed the uncle, don't think today that I have killed the king: I was not lying either time, my dear.

ANTIGONE: There are two Creons, are there?

CREON: Yes. And one of them takes precedence.

ANTIGONE: The king takes precedence, doesn't he? The uncle's been reported missing, but I begin to have an inkling where he's gone. Do you know where the spirit of Uncle Creon is? Here, entering into me! I'm Creon, Uncle Creon, the real Creon! Now I can do it!

CREON: Do what?

ANTIGONE: Now I *can* bury Polynices.

CREON (*in a strangled voice*): You have tried twice and failed.

ANTIGONE: I couldn't bear to die. *Then.* Creon, do you realize why Assface could bear to die?

CREON: He was a halfwit.

ANTIGONE: Maybe that helps. But Assface loved Polynices: that's the thing.

CREON: And you did not.

ANTIGONE: It was love and not high principles that gave Ass-face strength. I don't love Polynices, you are right. But there's *someone* I love.

CREON: You wanted to bury him *to spite me*. Even propelled by so much hatred you failed.

ANTIGONE: I didn't hate you enough. I did not hate you at all. I love you. I'll bury Polynices *because you want him buried and I love you.*

Pause.

CREON: In statecraft, child, decisions are commitments. The decisions that commit me were not made when Polynices died the other day but when he turned against us years ago. Of all moments, this is the least likely for me to change direction. The victory which was the goal of all my policy now lies within my grasp.

ANTIGONE (*slowly*): But what was it you said just now? You were asking if the burial of my brother could *really* bring about defeat, if leaving him unburied *really* could bring victory. "Is it *really* sure?" And if it isn't, "then all those measures which one knew were crimes were also grave miscalculations."

CREON (*recoiling*): That is a chance that both sides take in every war.

ANTIGONE: Then, Creon, what a load you're lifting from my soul! You are removing the final obstacle, the dreadful thought that by burying Polynices I'd be bringing defeat on Thebes and killing fellow Thebans . . . If this is quite unsure, my last excuse for hesitation's gone. I am going. Now. To the battlefield, where I will sprinkle on my brother's corpse a handful of earth, not for Freedom's sake, not for God's sake: for your sake.

CREON: That, no. (CREON *moves toward the door, stands blocking it, claps his hands twice for servants to come.*)

ANTIGONE: You would use force?

CREON (*bitterly*): Don't I always?

ANTIGONE: But now the luck, if that is what it is, is on my side. We're in my wing of the palace and no one is within earshot but two slaves of Oedipus—slaves of mine now—who will not come for you but who would gladly die for me. (ANTIGONE *claps her hands, as* CREON *had done.*)

The FIRST *and* SECOND SLAVES *enter and then do as bidden.*

Stand at the door. Don't let the king leave till I've been gone for half an hour.

CREON: Trapped! I am trapped! By you! How could this happen? It's another dream, surely, it can't be real!

Silence.

It's real. And you are Creon. The wrong Creon. Wrong but warmhearted. Then be warm to me and to Antigone. Look, King Creon kneels who never knelt before. (CREON *kneels.*) Antigone, the debate is done. I've nothing to say except: *don't do this thing. I beg you: don't! don't! don't!*

Silence.

ANTIGONE: We have to keep some part of ourselves, and that the center, secure, inviolate, even at the cost of deadly battle with the dragon wherever we may find him, even coiled round a corpse . . . Since it's *not* clear that the burial will lose Thebes the war and cost innumerable Theban lives: I must do what I must do.

As ANTIGONE *turns to go,* CREON *rises from his knees and starts forward as if to restrain her by force from going, but the* TWO SLAVES *seize him now by either arm.* ANTIGONE *turns, and across the room,* CREON *and* ANTIGONE *exchange a long look.* ANTIGONE *turns again and leaves.*

Gong.

FIRST SLAVE: For five minutes after she left, Creon threatened us: free him, or we would die.

SECOND SLAVE: After threats, five minutes of cajolery: Didn't we want to save the princess' life? We'd be rewarded with large sums of money.

FIRST SLAVE: Then five minutes of silence.

SECOND SLAVE: After which, Creon knew he could never over-take her.

FIRST SLAVE: All Thebes knows what happened next.

SECOND SLAVE: All Thebes and all Argos. All Greece maybe. For the flames from her pyre were seen across the Theban plain.

FIRST SLAVE: The people say they will be seen across the centuries when others shall say no and burn.

Gong.

a
time to live

For Herbert and Uta

PROLOGUE

The she-wolf howls, her sire squeals, her panther
Boy-friend practices bending bars of iron.
The frightened lamb clings to its mother, but
What can *she* do? Appeal to Great King Lion?
His Crown's dependent upon wolves and panthers.
Besides, he's fond of lamb chops. Only the
Sheepdog between sheep and jungle! And this
Sheepdog's more sheep than dog: they say that he
Gives wolves a wide berth and is predisposed
To minimize the panther boy-friend's rage.
He's old, tired, finished, and in awe of Lion.
Can he prove more dog than sheep at this stage?
We shall reply in the affirmative,
Say to the sleeping: Wake! To the dying, live!

CHARACTERS

STORY TELLER
PELEUS, *King of Thiotis and Achilles' father, aged 70*
ANDROMACHE, *Hector's widow*
HERMIONE, *Pyrrhus' wife*
MENELAUS, *Hermione's father*
PYRRHUS, *Achilles' son, aged 30*
ORESTES, *Agamemnon's son, aged 20*
AGAMEMNON, *King of Argos*

In the fortress town of Thiotis.

In the background, a throne room dimly lit; a king on his throne.

STORY TELLER (*in the foreground*): This is the story of an old king who was all set to die but changed his mind and decided to live. He was called Peleus and the place he was king of was a fortress town in the mountains of Greece called Thiotis. He had a famous son: Achilles. But that was earlier. Achilles was killed in the war; and now . . .

The lights go up on THE KING. *The* STORY TELLER *plays a* MESSENGER *reporting to him.*

MESSENGER: The war is over, Peleus.
THE KING (*rising*): The war?
MESSENGER: Is over.
THE KING: Praise be the gods! And my grandson Pyrrhus?
MESSENGER: Alive and well. He should be here by tomorrow. He will come straight to you.

THE KING: That I do not expect. First he must see his wife Hermione . . .

MESSENGER: He will come straight to you. Those were his words.

STORY TELLER: But before another day had gone by, a second messenger arrived.

THE KING: Pyrrhus is here?

SECOND MESSENGER (*also played by the* STORY TELLER): Not yet, King. I'm from Andromache.

THE KING: Andromache?

SECOND MESSENGER: You don't yet know? Ah yes, you thought your grandson was to be the messenger.

THE KING: Surely that is a Trojan princess' name?

SECOND MESSENGER: Know this then, King. Andromache has an infant child. The father is your grandson.

THE KING: Ah!

SECOND MESSENGER: And he has sent her on ahead to Greece. I am the officer in charge of mother and child. And I've placed her, as commanded, in the little Temple of Minerva . . .

THE KING: At the north end of the city?

SECOND MESSENGER (*nodding*): A hiding place till her affairs were set in order . . .

THE KING: To hide her from his wife Hermione . . . ?

SECOND MESSENGER: That was the aim, sire. But it's already failed.

THE KING: Hermione found out?

SECOND MESSENGER: She has combed the city. Must have got wind of things before we landed. And has been seen on her way to the Temple in the company of an older man . . .

THE KING: That will be her father Menelaus. He's living with Hermione . . .

SECOND MESSENGER: Come and save Andromache from them! Andromache and her son. They're unattended. A dozen of your Myrmidons should suffice.

THE KING: How do you know that they mean any harm? Couldn't it be a friendly visit . . . ?

SECOND MESSENGER: Friendly, sire? Preceded by spies and put through in such haste? Wives are a jealous lot . . .

THE KING: We must think the best of people, son. Hermione's childless. Naturally, she'll be jealous if her husband has a child by someone else. But she's not going to let jealousy run away with her . . .

SECOND MESSENGER: Will you come, sire? There's no time to waste.

THE KING: Yes, yes, of course. (*He starts to move.*)

SECOND MESSENGER: And with some Myrmidons?

THE KING: They won't be needed. But you can bring them. Come.

STORY TELLER: When Peleus set out, Hermione and her father hadn't reached the Temple yet. Andromache was alone there. Or rather, as so often of late, was with her baby, with whom, for consolation and to pass the time, she held imaginary conversations.

The Temple. ANDROMACHE *with her baby.*

ANDROMACHE: . . . and so Troy lost. (*Pause. In the pauses we imagine that the child speaks.*) Because Greece was so big, and Troy so small? Well argued, youngster! Yet you're wrong. Had Troy but been united . . . Troy had her traitors, son. It was one who opened the gates to the wooden horse, remember? So ends the story. You didn't understand it? Nor did I. (*Pause.*) Why did they come to Troy in the first place? Helen? Oh, there were other reasons. Even so, I'm like you: I do not understand it. How men can burn, burn, kill, kill, 'way beyond what they call "necessary"? (*Pause.*) Our family? That's just you and me. (*Pause.*) Yes, all. All slaughtered. Your grandfather Priam. Hector my husband. Our son Astyanax . . . No, baby, Hector was not your father . . . this too is hard to understand? . . . I'll say it's hard to understand, it's beyond all comprehension . . . ! (*Pause.*) Just how? Can I tell you? I guess I can, since you don't know the word. R . . . a . . . p . . . e . . . (*Pause.*) Rape is . . . war. War is . . . rape. A Greek called Pyrrhus raped me: you were

born. Facts of life! Those are the facts of . . . your life.
(*Pause.*) So I should hate him? You do argue well. But,
in Greece, reason *mis*leads. (*Pause.*) Do I love him? Does
he love me? Not that either. (*Pause.*) Revenge? I long for
no revenge. Yet neither is forgiveness on the map:
Pyrrhus and I are on the other side of love and hate . . .
on an expedition somewhere out beyond the old fidelities
and treacheries . . . (*Pause.*) You don't get that at all?
Nor should you, pet. But know this at least. Though
Pyrrhus can do nothing for *me,* he will try to help *you.*
This he has promised. This much I understand.

STORY TELLER: But now Hermione and Menelaus are heard
approaching, and a Temple priest hides Andromache in
an inner sanctum. (*He draws a curtain in front of* ANDROM-
ACHE.) For a while it seems that she will not be found.
But then . . .

Enter HERMIONE *and* MENELAUS.

MENELAUS: Another false trail: she simply isn't here.

HERMIONE: We've combed the whole city. She's got to be
here.

MENELAUS: We've looked in every room in this building.

HERMIONE: Wait a minute. Look at this. (*She strides over to
the curtain and draws it back.* ANDROMACHE *is revealed.
This time without child.*) Ah! (*A small cry of triumph.*)
Well, father?

MENELAUS: You've not checked who it is yet.

HERMIONE (*turning to* ANDROMACHE): I would know her in the
dark. Huh? You are Andromache, aren't you? Pyrrhus
mistress? I'm Hermione, his wife.

ANDROMACHE: What do you want?

HERMIONE: I'll ask the questions. You're hiding. Or being
hidden. Right? Why? You were very hard to find, but
I have spies. And determination: that if nothing else.
What's it all about, huh? Huh?

ANDROMACHE: I don't know how to answer you.

HERMIONE: Where's Pyrrhus?

ANDROMACHE: I . . . I do not think he's in Thiotis yet.

HERMIONE: Why are you here?

ANDROMACHE: I . . . was brought here.

HERMIONE: By whom?

ANDROMACHE: An officer.

HERMIONE: Prove it.

ANDROMACHE: He's not here now . . .

HERMIONE: Ah! Where is he? Where's he gone? What are you plotting? (*To her father.*) That'll be the one seen heading for the palace . . . (*She moves toward* ANDROMACHE.)

ANDROMACHE: Stop! Behind this line is sanctuary. You cannot touch me!

HERMIONE: Ha!

MENELAUS (*quickly*):   She's right, Hermione. That would be sanctuary.

HERMIONE: And, and?

MENELAUS: Well, of course, we wouldn't infringe on it. It's against Greek principles.

HERMIONE: This is a trick. (*To her rival.*) To hide your child . . . in the back there. (*Scrutinizing her.*) Not only glamorous but clever, huh?

ANDROMACHE: I think you'll find it hard to envy me.

HERMIONE (*furiously*):   Envy you? (*Dropping the fury.*) But why pretend? Sure I envy you . . .

MENELAUS: Hermione, you promised!

HERMIONE: Okay, *you* talk.

MENELAUS (*smoothly*):   First of all, you are Andromache? (*She nods.*) Well, in that case, there is so much, isn't there, that doesn't really need saying? Hermione feels she has been wronged: you can understand that. You feel you have been wronged: we can understand *that*. I myself was wronged before any of this started—the Helen and Paris business—remember? But you're too young. I'm too *old* to remember. Helen's back in Sparta now. That's why I'm here. I like a quiet life. I'm determined to *have* a quiet life. And can offer *you* one, too. (*He stops for effect.*)

ANDROMACHE: It seems unlikely.

MENELAUS: Here in Greece, yes. But you never wanted to be here in Greece, did you? You were dragged here as a slave. Well, we don't want you to be here, either. So our interests coincide. (*Stops again.*) Did you wish to say something?

ANDROMACHE: No.

MENELAUS: You can't get away, of course, on your own. You *can* get away with our help. We have come here for no other purpose than to proffer it.

Long pause.

HERMIONE: Our horsemen will take you to the coast. There they'll put you on a boat with enough gold to see you—and the kid—through the next ten years. On any of the islands you might pick to settle on.

Long pause.

MENELAUS: She needs a few minutes to get used to the idea. Let's withdraw, Hermione.

They start to withdraw.

ANDROMACHE: Stop! It isn't that. It's just that . . . Well, your plan would seem to be in my interest but . . .

HERMIONE: *But!* You refuse! You dare to refuse! Do you realize . . . ?

MENELAUS (*silencing her*): You don't believe us. Understandable. What guarantees do you want?

ANDROMACHE: I believe you. Even if I didn't, I'd have jumped at your offer, having nothing to lose, except that . . . (*She stops.*)

MENELAUS: Yes?

ANDROMACHE: I have to thank you for offering me what seems a way out but I . . . am not in a position to accept.

HERMIONE (*to* MENELAUS): What did I tell you? I told you no one could guess what they'd been up to, those two!

MENELAUS: And I warned you against having the whole thing out!

HERMIONE (*to* ANDROMACHE): I see it all. I saw it all from the start. You're lovers, you two! What's going on here is a rip-roaring affair! That child is the proof!

MENELAUS: Hermione!

HERMIONE (*mimicking*): "Hermione!" Menelaus, the great mediator! I've let you mediate, as you call it, and she's turned you down flat, just like I said she would!

ANDROMACHE (*in a low voice*): You can spare yourself much pain by not . . . inventing things that never, never happened.

HERMIONE: You were raped, I suppose? That's what they all say, the gals that get knocked up in wartime. (*Screaming.*) "Rape, I've been raped!" (*Quietly.*) A great alibi for hot pants.

ANDROMACHE: I was raped, Hermione, raped, raped, raped. No, don't shout! I am not protesting—now. Though this rape was no pleasanter than other rapes, and Pyrrhus and his friends had slaughtered my whole family.

HERMIONE (*loudly*): Now if it comes to atrocities, how about . . .

ANDROMACHE: No, no. I was raped. That is all.

HERMIONE (*stopped; and changing tone*): All right, my sly one, then explain to me why you no longer wish to escape this killing, burning, raping husband of mine?

ANDROMACHE (*quietly*): Do you love him?

HERMIONE: What business is that of yours? He's *my* husband, isn't he? Mine!

ANDROMACHE: You want to hold him?

HERMIONE: Of course!

ANDROMACHE: I don't. I do not love him. And I do not want him.

HERMIONE: Do you hate him at least?

ANDROMACHE: Not that either.

HERMIONE: I do. Love him and hate him. Want him and could break him if I don't get him . . . You aren't answering my question. If you neither loved nor hated this man, you'd be glad to run the other way at his approach.

ANDROMACHE: There is the child.

HERMIONE: You are taking your child with you.

ANDROMACHE: Into nothingness? No, no, the chances for him are better here . . . Pyrrhus said . . . (*She stops.*)

HERMIONE: Yes, yes?

ANDROMACHE: Why shouldn't you know? Pyrrhus said he would try to be of use to the child.

HERMIONE: What makes you believe such a monster of iniquity?

ANDROMACHE: It is his son, you see.

HERMIONE: Ha!

ANDROMACHE: Besides, he's very changed. In his whole attitude . . .

HERMIONE: I see, all right! I see, you bitch! And there's no need to rub it in!

MENELAUS: Hermione, if we get on *that* subject . . .

HERMIONE: He never gave *me* any son!

ANDROMACHE: Is that my fault?

HERMIONE: How do *I* know? I've heard you Trojan women are witches! But how would *I* know if you'd bewitched my womb, made me infertile?

ANDROMACHE: When did you last live with Pyrrhus? He's been in Troy!

HERMIONE: Yeah, with you, right? You yellow-skinned Trojan whore!

MENELAUS: Hermione!

ANDROMACHE: Pyrrhus hadn't even met me when he lived with you.

HERMIONE: How do I know you didn't start seducing him and sterilizing me years before you set eyes on either one of us?

MENELAUS: Hermione, all this will get you nowhere.

HERMIONE: Oh yeah? On the contrary, this is where the action starts. (*In a tone of military command.*) Come out of that damned sanctuary this minute. (*Silence. Stillness. Shrieking.*) Come out, you bitch, or I'll burn the place down! (*Silence. No moves. Quietly.*) Where's that kid of yours? (*Silence.*) Obviously in the back there. Father, you go get it. (*No action. She stamps her foot.*) Father, you will go and get it. (*No action.*) Things haven't changed much, have they, since you let Paris sling Mother across his shoulder and run off with her to Troy? (HERMIONE *crosses into sanctuary and into the inner room.*)

MENELAUS: Hermione, that is sanctuary!

HERMIONE *returns with the child and crosses so swiftly that* ANDROMACHE *is for the moment just left standing; then she follows* HERMIONE *out of the sanctuary to try to get the child back again.*

HERMIONE (*gives a triumphant cry*): Hah! (*Urgently to her father.*) Grab her! Grab her now if it's the last thing you ever do!

MENELAUS *now obeys orders. He is holding* ANDROMACHE, *and* HERMIONE *is holding the child, when a noise is heard from outside the Temple: orders to armed men to halt and stand at ease. Everyone is still transfixed as* THE KING *enters.*

THE KING: Good evening. What strange tableau is this? Daughter-in-law? Menelaus? You must be the Trojan princess, then?

ANDROMACHE *returns his gaze.* MENELAUS *lets her go, suddenly realizing what is going on.*

I am King Peleus, Pyrrhus' grandfather. Now what is happening?

Long pause.

ANDROMACHE: I took sanctuary over there. They broke in and snatched the child. I ran out to get him back.

THE KING: This cannot be true. Menelaus!

MENELAUS: I was against it.

THE KING: Then it didn't happen.

MENELAUS: The Trojan is exaggerating . . .

HERMIONE: Cut it out. Look, Peleus, sanctuary is for those who claim it, right? Did this child claim it?

THE KING: You are joking.

HERMIONE: I'm your grandson's wife but you haven't bothered to get to know me. Maybe you should have . . . No,

I'm not joking. This is a matter of life and death to me. Even at that I gave this Trojan witch the letter of the law. Greek law.

THE KING: Sanctuary's a law.

HERMIONE: For Greek citizens. She is a Trojan and a slave.

THE KING: Who placed her in sanctuary? Not herself? Princess?

ANDROMACHE: Pyrrhus' officer.

THE KING: There's the legality of it, Daughter-in-law. You must release her. Give her the child.

HERMIONE: Father, I propose we defy my father-in-law, and go ahead with our plan.

MENELAUS (*who has been looking through the window*): Hermione . . . may I speak to Hermione privately for a moment?

THE KING: Certainly.

MENELAUS (*to her, on one side*): Look, how many men did we bring out here?

HERMIONE: None.

MENELAUS: He has a dozen Myrmidons outside. Argument is useless.

HERMIONE (*going over to* THE KING): I'm sorry, Grandfather. I was out of my mind with jealousy. (*She gives* ANDROMACHE *the child.*)

THE KING: Granddaughter-in-law, you have been much provoked. I knew you'd be angry. But I also knew a Greek princess—one of *us*—would behave as a Greek princess. There are limits we will not transgress, are there not?

HERMIONE: Huh? Oh there are, there are.

THE KING: Andromache will be more . . . comfortable in the palace. (HERMIONE *gasps.*) When Pyrrhus returns, we shall work all things out. Be brave, Hermione. And patient, hm? You'll help her, Menelaus?

MENELAUS: Of course, of course.

THE KING: Then come, Andromache.

STORY TELLER: So Hermione went back to her house with her father, and King Peleus, with his Myrmidons, took

Andromache and her son to the Royal Palace. Sure enough. on the next day, Pyrrhus' arrival was announced by the King's personal valet, and there was a reunion of grandfather and grandson.

The STORY TELLER *now presents the* VALET *who stays on stage at one side during the whole scene, for reasons that are divulged later. The throne room as above.*

VALET: Your majesty, Prince Pyrrhus is on the stairs.

THE KING *rises from his throne, opening his arms to the* PRINCE *who embraces him on entering. Silence.*

THE KING (*looking at him*): You are changed, Grandson, really changed.

PYRRHUS: Not so yourself: the years have done nothing to you. (*Silence.*) Grandfather, don't be offended, but before we speak of anything else, tell me if what I've heard about Andromache is true: that Hermione tried to send her away, that you rescued her, that she is here in the palace . . . ?

THE KING: It is all true.

PYRRHUS: Then I am very greatly in your debt.

THE KING: Tush. I am about to be in yours, or so I hope.

PYRRHUS: What is there *I* can do?

THE KING: Already, when Achilles left for Troy, he agreed that, on the day of his return, he'd take this crown of mine and let me retire. My constant dream has been the little farm I'd have, my interests confined to cows and hens and turkeys. No more human beings, they're too much for me! *Living* is too much for me. Yes, let me admit I want to die—by pleasant inches. A hard place, Greece, to live in; but, to die in, perfect. One can just fade into our soft and sunlit landscape . . . Well then, Grandson, since Achilles *won't* return, will *you* do . . . what *he* was going to do?

PYRRHUS: Ascend the throne—immediately?

THE KING: That's right. (*Silence.*) You are silent?

PYRRHUS: I'm so thrilled you think that I could fill Achilles'

place—and yours. But you don't know much about me
. . . there are things I now believe . . .

THE KING: About the war, oh, yes, I know!

PYRRHUS: But I fought it. Carried out orders to the end.

THE KING: But finally without belief. With the reverse belief.
You believe Troy was right and Greece was wrong.

PYRRHUS: Troy was the victim; Greece was the aggressor.

THE KING: You no longer believe it was fought for Menelaus'
honor . . .

PYRRHUS: Let alone for the honor of Greece. No, no, it was
fought, without any doubt, for the aggrandizement of
Agamemnon.

THE KING: "A victory of the big over the little, of the up-to-
date against the old-fashioned . . ."

PYRRHUS: And you agree to all of this?

THE KING: Put it this way: I am afraid you're right. I'm
certainly *afraid*!

PYRRHUS: Go on.

THE KING: Is it true that Agamemnon always held back
Argive troops, sending the men of other cities into battle?

PYRRHUS: Exactly so. When he gets back from Troy—he's
not back yet—his army will be intact, his weapons the
best in the world—the rest of us, old crocks in rusty
armor.

THE KING: He expects . . .

PYRRHUS: That the cities of Greece will fall one by one into
his pocket, our Thiotis among them.

THE KING: And will they?

PYRRHUS: What do *you* think? What would you do—if you
stayed on as King?

THE KING: Stave off the evil day. Reach some accommodation.
Avoid violence at all costs.

PYRRHUS: D'you know then what you're doing when you give
your crown to me?

THE KING: You too would avoid war, I hope . . .

PYRRHUS: I would defy Agamemnon. Defend our independence.

THE KING: But that is suicide!

PYRRHUS: How many men has he?

THE KING: At least 5,000.

PYRRHUS: And we?

THE KING: Just the 500 Myrmidons.

PYRRHUS: Just, eh? You don't count the people of Thiotis? A little people fighting for its own works miracles.

THE KING: But our people only number a couple of thousand.

PYRRHUS: *Free* men.

THE KING: Free men. Of course. The rest are Trojans. Slaves.

PYRRHUS: You never thought of mobilizing *them*?

THE KING: No one has ever done a thing like that!

PYRRHUS: Then I shall be the first.

THE KING: You scare me more and more. (*Pause.*) Yet it's a stirring vision . . .You say you *will* do this. It's settled then . . . you'll take the crown?

PYRRHUS: On one condition, yes.

THE KING: What is it?

PYRRHUS: That you legitimize Molossus.

THE KING: Your son?

PYRRHUS: And your great-grandson.

Pause.

THE KING: I thought you'd changed the subject but you haven't. Your son's a . . . Trojan slave. But he's also . . . Achilles' grandson, a Greek prince among Greek princes. With him as your heir, you would be offering Thiotis that novel kind of unity you spoke of . . .

PYRRHUS: I'm glad you see that. You will go ahead?

Pause.

THE KING: I'd rather *you* did it. When you are king.

PYRRHUS: Thiotian law on that point reads . . .

THE KING: Ah yes. No king here may legitimize his own natural children.

PYRRHUS: So it *must* be you.

THE KING: And then you'll take the crown?

PYRRHUS: Forthwith.

THE KING (*after a pause*): And yet I can't believe that they're that bad.

PYRRHUS: What's this? Who's not all that bad?

THE KING: Agamemnon. His allies. The powers that be in Greece . . .

PYRRHUS: Ten years of Trojan War . . .

THE KING: Yes, yes, but they believed that it was right . . . even I believed that, in the beginning, even you did . . .

PYRRHUS: People who never learn . . .

THE KING: I can't believe Agamemnon would take over all of Greece. Would attack Thiotis.

PYRRHUS: I haven't asked you to.

THE KING: For me to legitimize this half-Trojan child—you yourself have explained . . .

PYRRHUS: Tell me, Grandfather, do you hate Trojans?

THE KING: No, no.

PYRRHUS: Feel that there's something strange about them . . . their yellowish skin . . .

THE KING: And slanting eyes? No, I don't mind. Though it's funny how our half-breeds always seem a hundred per cent Oriental . . .

PYRRHUS: Then legitimize Molossus.

THE KING (*after a pause*): And if I do? Hermione will challenge my authority.

PYRRHUS: Scared of my wife?

THE KING: You should have seen her, heard her in the Temple . . . Working on Agamemnon's very brother . . .

PYRRHUS: Yes, yes: there is danger here. What can you hope to do by bucking danger? Sooner or later one must take a stand.

THE KING: I can make sure it's later. Why shouldn't that be my final contribution?

PYRRHUS: Postponement of the inevitable?

THE KING: Giving you time to make it . . . not inevitable.

PYRRHUS: *How* would you do this? Do you see a way?

THE KING: Yes. Have the child legitimized by someone else. Someone with more prestige. Religious prestige at that. Then we have something Hermione cannot challenge.

PYRRHUS: Like who?

THE KING: The High Priest of Apollo.

PYRRHUS: But he's in Delphi.

THE KING: In three days you can be there and back again: it's worth it.

PYRRHUS: You want *me* to go there? Now?

THE KING: While I stand guard here over your son.

PYRRHUS: Hm. It's ingenious. Evasive but ingenious . . . Grandfather, won't you think again and do it yourself?

THE KING *shakes his head.*

That would be *my* way.

THE KING: And this is mine. I am *incapable* of what you suggest. Too small, too timid, and too tired. So let me end my kingship, not with a deed that leads to violence, but with a kind of diplomatic coup. A *fait accompli* that they dare not challenge.

PYRRHUS: Since otherwise you refuse . . .

THE KING: There's my grandson. In three days you'll be back.

PYRRHUS: Then it's farewell . . .

THE KING: Say rather: till we meet again.

They embrace. PYRRHUS *starts to go. Returns.*

PYRRHUS: My journey must be secret, hm?

THE KING: Yes, yes, don't leave till nightfall.

PYRRHUS: All those precautions were taken with Andromache. Hermione found her.

THE KING: She won't lay hands on *you*. Even if her spies do see you. Things haven't gone *that* far!

PYRRHUS (*briskly*): I got through ten years of war: I can take care of myself. The person to protect is Andromache . . . and my son.

THE KING: Five hundred Myrmidons stand guard over them.

PYRRHUS: Then may all be for the best. (*He leaves the throne room. The* VALET *slips out by another door.*)

STORY TELLER: By nightfall Pyrrhus was ready and with a single servant set out toward Delphi. Silently Hermione and her father retraced their steps from the Temple of Minerva.

HERMIONE *at home. A long table. She and her father at each end. They eat in silence for a while.*

HERMIONE: Cousin Orestes. Why's he in Thiotis?

MENELAUS: Don't ask.

HERMIONE: As bad as that?

MENELAUS: Worse.

HERMIONE: Howdya mean that?

MENELAUS: Well, I mean, why are *we* here?

HERMIONE: Who?

MENELAUS: You and me.

HERMIONE: I married Pyrrhus.

MENELAUS: Why?

HERMIONE: Had to get out of Sparta somehow. Didn't have a war to go off to like you.

MENELAUS: Did I go back to Sparta? *(Pause to eat.)* Why not?

HERMIONE: Because Helen's back.

MENELAUS: Helen and a hundred minions of brother Agamemnon. We both came here for the same reason, you and I: to get away from it all. To relax for a change. Be left in peace for a change. Curl up in a corner and take a pleasant snooze . . . But the sonofabitch always was power crazy, and now he's coming here.

HERMIONE: Uncle Agamemnon? Coming here? When?

MENELAUS: At that, he may drop in on us in person on his way home from the wars . . . but that's not what I meant.

HERMIONE: Explain yourself.

MENELAUS: I meant he's taking over all of Greece. Bit by bit. Sparta—he has it already, or I wouldn't be in Thiotis. But now he has his eye on this city.

HERMIONE *(after another pause for eating)*: That's Uncle Agamemnon. But I asked about Cousin Orestes.

MENELAUS: And I said: don't.

HERMIONE *(eats again)*: But I did.

MENELAUS: Well, the cousin's the son of the uncle, isn't he?

Pause.

HERMIONE: You know something you're not telling me.

MENELAUS: Because I don't want to tell even myself.

HERMIONE: Spill it.

MENELAUS: Why not put your spies on him for a change?

HERMIONE: Orestes? Maybe I will now you've got me interested.

MENELAUS: He hopes to play the Trojan horse here. Only it's not a horse this time. It's something called Argive Industries—on Main Street.

HERMIONE: But that's just a trading mission. I've seen the place.

MENELAUS: What do they trade in? What industries?

HERMIONE: How do *I* know?

MENELAUS: It's a gimmick for bringing Argive hatchet men into Thiotis. Against the day . . .

Pause.

HERMIONE: You're paranoid.

MENELAUS: Put your spies on him. Better still, put yourself on him, he's sweet on you, isn't he?

HERMIONE: What gave you that impression? He hardly knows me.

MENELAUS: But at the Chamber of Commerce Ball he . . .

HERMIONE: Oh, that, yes he . . .

MENELAUS: Walked clear across the dance floor with his eyes fixed on you, burning with . . .

HERMIONE: That was his word. Came striding across. I hardly knew who it was. Then says: "I love you. It's burning me up."

MENELAUS (*upset to hear this*):   Now, Hermione, the day you get mixed up with Orestes is the end of all our dreams for each other . . .

HERMIONE: Dreams for each other, hell . . .

MENELAUS: That we were talking about. Getting away from it all. Finding a little safety at last, comfort, peace, and quiet . . .

The VALET *enters.*

Who are you?

HERMIONE: Good gods, it's old Peleus' personal valet!

MENELAUS: How, in Heaven's name, did you get in here?

HERMIONE: Go easy, Father. I pay him.

MENELAUS: He's one of your . . . ?

HERMIONE (*to* VALET):   What is it?

VALET: Pyrrhus has left the palace again. Left at nightfall. For Delphi . . .

MENELAUS: Pyrrhus' movements no longer hold any interest for us.

HERMIONE: Wait a minute. What would he be going to Delphi for?

VALET: He asked the King to make his son legitimate.

HERMIONE: What?

VALET: The King wouldn't, but said the High Priest of Apollo would . . .

HERMIONE: What? Would what?

VALET: Make his son legitimate.

HERMIONE: You dare to say that twice? Get out! (*He leaves. She shouts after him.*) I shall have you horse-whipped! (*Long pause.*) Legitimate! Then this miserable Trojan brat will be king here one day! And that Trojan whore will be queen in less than three days!

MENELAUS: There was nothing about divorce . . .

HERMIONE: Divorce, marriage, *pfui!* The mother of the heir to the throne is queen!

MENELAUS: But it doesn't make sense. Why the High Priest? Old Peleus could have done it . . .

HERMIONE: I'd have challenged that, and he knows it. I'd never have let him get away with it. Sly old biddy. I'd have made him eat his words!

MENELAUS: That's right. But we can't challenge Apollo!

Silence. MENELAUS *seems stunned,* HERMIONE *driven wild . . . she paces the room.*

HERMIONE: We should have cut them down right then and there.

MENELAUS: What's that? Who're you talking about?

HERMIONE: The Trojan and her bastard. In the Temple. When we had them at our mercy!

MENELAUS: They were in sanctuary!

HERMIONE: "They were in sanctuary!" You're another old biddy. You and Peleus are a pair. "There are limits we will not transgress." All hypocrisy anyway! You go out and slaughter 1,000 men at a throw on your battlefields. Why not one whore and one brat?

MENELAUS: Anyhow, it's too late now.

HERMIONE: Too late. You have spent your life permitting disasters and then whimpering "Too Late, Too Late!" (*She paces.*) How long does it take to get to Delphi? (*Pause.*) You let those two slip through your fingers. Now you've let Pyrrhus slip through your fingers.

MENELAUS: Slip through *my* fingers? What could I do with him anyway? Pack *him* off to an island with a bag of gold?

HERMIONE: How long does it take to get to Delphi?

MENELAUS: Best part of two days.

HERMIONE: And when did that fellow say Pyrrhus left?

MENELAUS: At nightfall.

HERMIONE: That's what I mean. He can be overtaken.

MENELAUS: And I said: "Shall I pack him off to-an island with a bag of gold?"

HERMIONE: Andromache and the child are guarded by the Myrmidons. The child becomes legitimate the minute Pyrrhus reaches Delphi. Therefore: Pyrrhus must not reach Delphi.

MENELAUS: Nothing could possibly dissuade him . . .

HERMIONE: Dissuade my foot, this is a . . .

MENELAUS: You wouldn't . . . kidnap your own husband?

HERMIONE: No. Not a bad idea, but we're beyond that stage. No, look, Menelaus. Would you like the chance to completely rehabilitate yourself? You lost your self-respect ten years ago when you stood by and called "Too Late" after the fleeing Paris. And don't give me that gook about why you didn't go back to Sparta. I know why you didn't go back to Sparta. You're a famous laughingstock there, you're folklore, you're source material for Greek comedy. But I can now offer you a chance to recoup. The last you're ever gonna have.

MENELAUS: You are not suggesting that I . . . I . . . I . . .

HERMIONE: Be a man. Yeah: that you be a man. For the first time in your life. Kill Pyrrhus.

MENELAUS: Hermione . . .

HERMIONE: KILL PYRRHUS. KILL PYRRHUS. KILL PYRRHUS.

Long pause.

MENELAUS: You are not being fair to me, I . . .

HERMIONE: What, what? You are letting *this* chance slip, too, you are determined to make the name Menelaus a byword for . . .

MENELAUS: Okay, I'm afraid. Supposing I wasn't. Would that make it right? How about that quiet life we came here for . . .

HERMIONE: You have killed men. With very little reason. Kill one now with very much reason.

MENELAUS: They were Trojans. That I killed. We don't kill Greeks!

HERMIONE: Oh we don't, eh? Well what was that you told me about Uncle Agamemnon? Is he hoping to take over all of Greece without spilling one drop of blood?

MENELAUS: But I'm against what he's doing, I . . .

HERMIONE: Yeah, you're against it. And you're against stopping Pyrrhus. *You* are. Menelaus the famous cuckold. But I bet I know who'd be for it.

MENELAUS (*quickly*):   No, no, don't go to Orestes. Avenging yourself on your husband is one thing. Avenging yourself on a whole city . . . which has done you no harm . . .

HERMIONE: Fine, fine. Let's test your sincerity on that. If you want to stop me going to Orestes, if you want to "save Thiotis," then do it yourself. Come on, Menelaus, get it up for once—before it's too late!

Long pause.

MENELAUS: I think you're going right out of your mind, Hermione.

HERMIONE (*turning on him savagely*):   Oh I am, am I? Then you go right out of my house!

MENELAUS: Now? Are you serious? In the middle of supper?

HERMIONE: Yeah. Pack your little suitcase and go! Get out of my life for good and all.

MENELAUS: Back to Sparta?

HERMIONE (*mimicking*): "Back to Sparta"! Back to Hades!
Go where you damn please, but go!

MENELAUS: Hermione . . . (*But he finds nothing to say; and
leaves.*)

HERMIONE: I must find Orestes.

STORY TELLER: It was early next morning before she found
him. Though the sun had only just risen, he was at his
place of work on Main Street. In the window the sign
read: ARGIVE INDUSTRIES. Hermione introduced herself to
the man behind the counter as Orestes' cousin.

*Back room of an office. A big plan of the city on the wall.
On a table, what seems to be another plan, with pins
stuck in it—the pins that generals stick in maps when
planning a campaign.* ORESTES *is there, toying with the
pins.*

ORESTES (*shouting to the front room*): Well, send her in, this
gal that says she's my cousin.

HERMIONE *is brought in by Orestes' man, played by the*
STORY TELLER.

Hey, but it *is* my cousin. Hey, now, wait a minute, why
would *you* come *here?* At this hour? Alone? (*She nods. He
looks at the man for verification, and the latter nods too.*)
Unless you have a posse a couple of blocks away? Shall I
have him look?

HERMIONE: There isn't time.

ORESTES: Oh?

HERMIONE: And cut out the play acting. I know why you are
in this town.

ORESTES: As President of Argive Industries, of course.

HERMIONE: As Commander-in-Chief of your father's Trojan
horse.

ORESTES: No comment. But if that were the truth, you and
Menelaus would regard me as your arch enemy. I know
why you two are in this town. What's your problem?

HERMIONE: My husband has returned from the wars with a
Trojan mistress and a brat. His brat.

ORESTES: That's no news to me. But so have many other Greek husbands.

HERMIONE: He now proposes to legitimize the child.

ORESTES: Huh? That's . . . unusual. And has, um, far-reaching consequences . . . You have no children? (HERMIONE *shakes her head.*) So the Trojan child is Pyrrhus' heir? (*She nods.*) A very shrewd political move on Pyrrhus' part.

HERMIONE: Is that all you have to say?

ORESTES: What more *should* I say?

HERMIONE: Pyrrhus has only just set out for Delphi. He could be stopped. Liquidated.

ORESTES: Oh? So you're looking for an assassin? (*Pause.*) And your fertile imagination has cast me for the role?

HERMIONE: As Thiotis' worst enemy.

ORESTES: Oh, but my instructions . . . I should say: if your premise were correct, I'm sure my instructions would be strictly to avoid such incidents at this stage in the game.

HERMIONE: Send your man out.

ORESTES: What? (*Pause.*) Well, delighted. (*Shows his man the door.*)

HERMIONE: You said you loved me. That night.

ORESTES: Hm? Oh, yes. And I did. Burned like a furnace for you.

HERMIONE: So I thought I could call on you . . .

ORESTES: But furnaces don't stay alight without fuel.

HERMIONE: What? It's not true anymore?

ORESTES: No.

HERMIONE: Oh. In that case I'd better be going. (*Starts to go.*)

ORESTES: Wait a minute. Sometimes a furnace can be re-lit, huh?

HERMIONE (*turning*): Can this one?

Pause.

ORESTES: Yes, I think so. (*Scrutinizing her.*) I know so. (*Pause.*) You mean, you would if . . . (*Pause.*) I see. (*Pause.*) Suppose this . . . deed were done, what next?

HERMIONE: Next?

ORESTES: Politically. As you have guessed, my mission to

Thiotis is . . . political as well as economic . . .

HERMIONE (*flushing*): Is that your answer?

ORESTES: Agamemnon would be very angry if he knew I'd said that much—what's more he may show up here one day soon—another top secret by the way . . . See how I trust you . . .

HERMIONE: Look, young man. I've been a respectable wife. Not a good one, but a respectable one. No adultery, you understand. I now go to the lengths of actually offering . . .

ORESTES: I appreciate that. I *shall* appreciate it . . . at the right moment . . . But you come to see me entirely by surprise, in office hours . . . Sex isn't everything, you know . . . (HERMIONE *snorts*.) What happens once this murder is committed?

HERMIONE: I'm not concerned with that.

ORESTES: I am. Suppose the old King himself makes this bastard legitimate?

HERMIONE: Peleus? You obviously don't know him. He's going to get the scare of his life. And he was good and scared even before.

ORESTES: He will collapse, and leave Andromache and her child to us?

HERMIONE: He'll have no option.

ORESTES: And I myself?

HERMIONE: I . . . have already said—good gods, do you just want to humiliate me?

ORESTES: I get *you*. I get a torrid love affair out if it. Great. I like torrid love affairs. And the night I propositioned you I was definitely in the mood. But, cousin, I am not going to do . . . what you ask . . . for the honor of a wild weekend in a roadhouse with you.

HERMIONE: You're not?

ORESTES: No, I'm not.

HERMIONE (*wearily*): Then, once again, I think I should be going . . .

ORESTES: I don't. I think you should be staying.

HERMIONE (*turning*): You confuse me.

ORESTES: We can make so much more than love out of this

thing. Both of us. The death of Pyrrhus is not the end.
It is the beginning.

HERMIONE: Okay, Andromache and her son must also go.

ORESTES: All right. And who must *come?* Pyrrhus must have
a successor. That's the nub of the whole thing, right?
So, if not this Trojan infant, then who? Who? (*He stands
up. Her face shows dawning recognition.*) That's right.
Me. But don't you feel left out. You're not. You're my
way in. Queen of Thiotis. The man to whom you give
your hand in marriage will be Thiotis' king.

HERMIONE (*weakly*):   Marriage? I said nothing of marriage . . .

ORESTES: No, that was the weakness of your position. You're
not very political, are you, little lady? You're gonna have
to be. Because you're gonna have to sit on that throne.
Next to me. Always. Uniting the old Thiotis (*He points
to her.*) with the new. (*He points to himself.*) Is it a deal?

HERMIONE (*dizzy, one hand to her forehead*):   Will you . . .
murder Pyrrhus?

ORESTES: Will you . . . marry me?

HERMIONE *gasps, tries to speak.*

Then I'll *execute* Pyrrhus: that is the word Father will
use. Pyrrhus was an enemy of the people and had to be
executed. Big deal. There will be "repercussions" throughout the Peninsula, and everywhere Trojans will stay
Trojans, slaves will stay slaves.

HERMIONE: There is no time to lose . . .

ORESTES: I must get the boys together—Argive Industries
goes into action! When did Pyrrhus leave?

HERMIONE: At nightfall.

ORESTES: Hm. And we must catch him before he reaches
Delphi?

HERMIONE: At all costs.

ORESTES: If it can be done, we'll do it . . .

They start out; stop in the doorway.

You're sure about old Peleus being no problem after-
wards?

HERMIONE: Forget it.

ORESTES: Then get ready.

HERMIONE *is astonished.*

Yes, you're coming with us. And when Agamemnon gets to this burg, we'll be its king and queen.

STORY TELLER: Meanwhile, in the palace, Peleus placed Andromache and her child in a room apart. And the grandfather waited for the grandson twenty-four hours. And again twenty-four hours. Toward the end of the third day he sent for Andromache.

The throne room of the Royal Palace as at the beginning of the play. Again, THE KING *is on the throne.* ANDROMACHE *is just entering.*

THE KING: I have been silent for two days and more. Tonight, however, Pyrrhus will return. In triumph. Yes, a kind of triumph . . . for us all.

ANDROMACHE: Where has he gone?

THE KING: He told you he would "try to help the child." At my behest he's gone to Delphi where the High Priest of Apollo

ANDROMACHE *stops up her ears.*

. . . are you not listening, Andromache?

ANDROMACHE: I dare not! Oh, I dare not hope so much!

THE KING: . . . where the High Priest of Apollo must by now have made your son legitimate.

ANDROMACHE (*who hears this through her hands*):   Ah! (*It is a piercing cry of joy.*)

THE KING: He thus becomes the heir to this throne.

ANDROMACHE: Now I can die in peace.

THE KING (*smiling*):   Dying in peace is my job! I can yield the throne to Pyrrhus. You have good cause to live.

ANDROMACHE: I still can't quite believe it.

THE KING: Greece is not all bad, Andromache.

ANDROMACHE: I see that now. I would never have believed Hermione would have agreed to this!

THE KING: To what, my child?

ANDROMACHE: Letting my child live—as a prince—a Greek.

THE KING: Agreed to it?!

ANDROMACHE: I have misjudged her.

THE KING: Princess, she did not *agree* to it. We did not tell her.

ANDROMACHE: She does not know? What if she finds out before it's done? What if she did find out?

THE KING: We thought of that, child. And there is nothing she could do.

ANDROMACHE: Nothing she could do? Don't you know women?

THE KING: Princess, please!

ANDROMACHE: A woman who believes herself cheated, outwitted, defeated, humiliated—there is nothing she will not do!

THE KING: You come from the wilds of Asia Minor. This is Greece. Hellas! Our women are not savages.

ANDROMACHE: Your men are. Forgive me, gentle King, but it is true. You've lived protected up on this hillside. Protected even from Greece!

THE KING (*testily*):   Let's not re-fight the Trojan War, my child . . .

ANDROMACHE: How many soldiers did Pyrrhus take to Delphi?

THE KING: Why, none. It was a secret journey. The Myrmidons are all here—guarding you, my lady.

ANDROMACHE: Secret! A secret that her spies could break wide open!

THE KING: I know my Greeks, Andromache. Men *and* women. Very well, they are wicked. So are other mortals. But all Greek history hasn't gone for naught. No, no, we led the way. It was for us to show the world how to set limits on this wickedness. To establish rule of law and say: thus far and no farther.

ANDROMACHE: But I am a barbarian. I fear for Pyrrhus' life. Can't you send soldiers *now*?

THE KING: Tush, child. Pyrrhus may walk in at any moment, bearing the precious document in his hand!

ANDROMACHE: Send for Hermione. Find out *if* she knows. And, if she does, what she has done. She did break sanctuary!

THE KING: Hermione has broken . . . some of our laws. But the law of life? That is a far cry surely from anything she's done. To murder a husband? No, no, there she would draw the line.

ANDROMACHE: And if she didn't?

THE KING (*provoked*): She'd never be able to bring it off anyway!

ANDROMACHE: Alone, no. But think of her connections . . .

THE KING: Her father's against *anything* that makes trouble, he . . .

ANDROMACHE: What if she ventured further? Is not Orestes rumored to be around? Agamemnon himself . . .

THE KING (*his temper rising further*): You are a Trojan! How dare you presume to set Greek against Greek!

ANDROMACHE: Pyrrhus told me the time was coming for just that!

THE KING (*boiling over*): Pyrrhus told you . . . ! (*As the rage recedes.*) Ah yes, that's Pyrrhus' notion. Such may be the new age that's dawning now. I don't belong in it. Nor does Hermione. Even Agamemnon, even Orestes would draw the line at . . . And so we counter them with caution, prudence, at the worst with cunning, do all with gentleness.

Enter Pyrrhus' SERVANT, *played by the* STORY TELLER.

ANDROMACHE: Pyrrhus' servant!

PELEUS (*staring at the dust-covered* SERVANT *whose message is in his face*): What is the matter, young man?

SERVANT: Prince Pyrrhus has been . . . (*He stops.*)

THE KING: Yes, yes?

SERVANT: Assassinated.

ANDROMACHE: Oh, no, no!

THE KING: Tell us what happened.

SERVANT: We had almost reached Delphi. We emerged from the forest and could see Mount Parnassus in the distance. At that point there is a chapel where travelers pause to give thanks or just to rest. And Pyrrhus bade me stand on horseback on a nearby hillock while he prayed. He was already praying when I heard a sound. Before I could make a move, several dozen hooded horsemen had encircled the chapel. I was 'way outside the circle. All carried spears save three who dismounted, crept up behind the praying Pyrrhus, and threw a net over him. They must have known their trade, for when he jumped up, with a flick of the wrist they turned the net and him, and he was upside down, kicking and struggling, but helpless as an overturned tortoise. As suddenly the net was roped shut, they hung it and him by the rope-end from the nearest branch. Then, O King—but this you must not hear . . . (*He stops.*)

THE KING: Go on. Go on.

SERVANT: The hooded horsemen all moved past the body and, as each passed, he drove his spear into the helpless Pyrrhus. Some lances went right through him, leaving their points dripping with his blood. Others hung from his flesh, or dropped with a splash in the lake of blood beneath. Two of the hooded figures stood apart, making no move till the whole bloody ritual was over. Then they removed their hoods.

THE KING *lets out a great cry of anguish and recognition.*

It was Orestes and Hermione. Orestes spoke. "Executioners, your anonymity will be preserved. And let what you have done stand as a warning. Never shall Greece be ruled by Trojans! Never shall Trojans be Greek citizens!" Hermione spoke: "I am Queen of Thiotis, and I take, for husband and for King, Orestes, son of Agamemnon, King of Argos." Orestes dipped his hand in the blood of Pyrrhus and with his finger wrote the A of Argos on her forehead . . . I fled then, King, and have come straight to you. Orestes and Hermione will follow. You must flee.

A noise outside.

Is it too late? (*He goes to the window to look. A sound of drums.*) But this is not Orestes' gang! This is . . . Agamemnon is already in the palace . . . !

Sound of military escort in the corridor just outside the throne room. AGAMEMNON *enters.* THE KING *is prostrate and does not look up as the King of Argos starts speaking.*

AGAMEMNON (*taking in the scene, and addressing himself to the others*): He has already heard, then? Ah yes, the dreadful news has felled him like an oak tree in a storm. Peleus, this is Agamemnon. I want you to know how vehemently I repudiate this deed. I knew nothing of it, before. I condemn it, after. (PELEUS *is motionless.*) I am a warrior-king, Peleus, and idle tongues have called me predatory, but let the world take note that I condemn crime when I see it, yes, even in my own son and niece. Nor would I intrude upon you at this hour merely to talk. I bring help too—help above all. Orestes and his men are headed here. I have no soldiers with me, cannot promise to control him. Instead, I'll save you from him now—and make you safe forever. It's true, is it not, old Peleus, you have longed for rest—for nothing else indeed —these many years? Rest and a little comfort. I'm giving you my winter palace on the Isle of Delos where you can live as carefree as the birds. My men can take you there at once: on horseback to the coast, then, in my boat . . . two days at most to Delos.

THE KING (*raising his head for the first time*): Alas, I can scarcely think . . . I need time . . . Is this Agamemnon?

AGAMEMNON: It is indeed. And I'm no ogre, hm? But time there is not. I must snatch you from the clutches of this mad son of mine . . .

THE KING: Such kindness, kindness . . . I was just telling—

this is Andromache, sire—I was just telling her we're bad, we Greeks, we're really wicked, yet there's a limit . . . and you know . . .

AGAMEMNON: Exactly so. I'd keep disaster within certain bounds.

THE KING: What do you think, Andromache? For me, it really doesn't matter—but for you, for the child?

AGAMEMNON (*cutting in but not loudly*): This must be settled between you and me, Peleus.

THE KING: I am . . . inclined to do as you suggest . . . Will you get ready, Andromache . . .

AGAMEMNON: No, no, we can't take her: it is just you.

THE KING: Just me? Then I'm not interested.

AGAMEMNON (*slowly*): We won't lay hands on her or on her son. (ANDROMACHE *gives a stifled cry.*) That is a promise— from Agamemnon, King of Argos, King of All Greek Kings.

PELEUS *has been coming out of the coma into which the terrible news had thrown him. He starts now to move about uneasily.*

Confirming your own view—that there's a limit—beyond which Greece won't go. (*Silence.*) Here's my promise. (AGAMEMNON *offers his hand.* PELEUS *does not take it.*) What's the matter, Peleus?

THE KING: That I'm an idiot.

AGAMEMNON: What's that?

THE KING: That I'm an idiot, that I'll never learn. Look. I thought Hermione wouldn't pass the bounds. Thought? I was *convinced* with all my heart and soul. And then what happened?

AGAMEMNON: I'm not some jealous girl. The case is different . . .

THE KING: You say if *I* stay here you cannot answer for the consequences, you can't handle your Orestes . . . But if *she* stays here, you answer for the consequences but totally, with a solemn promise . . .

AGAMEMNON: Look, Peleus, my patience is not inexhaustible. Like the god from the machine in our old plays, I offer you a happy end. Are you turning it down?

THE KING: Yes.

AGAMEMNON: Now why *is* that?

THE KING: I do not trust you. You would break your word.

AGAMEMNON: Now, Peleus, Andromache and her son will not be saved this way. Nor will you. Do you know what will happen? Orestes' scheme will just go through as planned. Before the day is out, Peleus—before the day is out . . . maybe in the next hour—they will be here; all three of you will be executed; Orestes and Hermione will be King and Queen.

THE KING (*to* ANDROMACHE *and* SERVANT): Leave us. How many men have you brought here?

AGAMEMNON: A dozen at most.

THE KING: And Orestes' hooded gang—and other Trojan horsemen in my city?

AGAMEMNON: Several dozen more.

THE KING: I have 500 Myrmidons right here in this building.

Pause.

AGAMEMNON: Are you threatening me?

THE KING: Yes.

AGAMEMNON: Well, that is merely ludicrous. Ludicrous!

THE KING: Not at all. I am pointing out that you *cannot* take the three of us and kill us.

AGAMEMNON: Because, now, you're threatening resistance. Well and good. Resist today with your 500 peasants and tomorrow you'll confront Argos.

THE KING: Ah! You're *not* against Orestes. You stand *with* him! You have been *lying* to me, King Agamemnon!

AGAMEMNON: I was not behind his crime. I'm against that sort of thing. But now it's an accomplished fact . . .

THE KING: If your sons will only commit your crimes for you, you're quite prepared to reap the benefits?

AGAMEMNON (*sharply*): You talk like Pyrrhus!

Pause.

THE KING: Thank you. That's a beginning anyway. Now I must *act* like Pyrrhus.

AGAMEMNON: Resist. Go ahead. Be pigheaded if you must. Get carried away with the oratory of subversion. And then what? Just this, Peleus. YOU WILL LOSE. YOU WILL LOSE. The gods are on the side of the big battalions.

THE KING: And 5,000 is big—against 500.

AGAMEMNON: Exactly.

THE KING (*as Pyrrhus' words come to mind*): But a small people, fighting for its own, can achieve miracles.

AGAMEMNON: The Trojan people didn't.

THE KING: They were divided. Some sold out to you. How many Thiotians in your son's Trojan horse? (*Silence.*) None. We can unite against you. The whole population will fight. Even, Agamemnon, the slaves.

AGAMEMNON: Trojans—who have just seen their homes and families destroyed by Greeks will fight for no Greek city —I know the Trojans . . .

THE KING: As enemies. We shall approach them as friends.

AGAMEMNON: By asking them to die for you?

THE KING: By giving them a choice: to leave—or to fight . . . for themselves—for a city that will be theirs as well as ours.

AGAMEMNON: Pah! The whole ruling caste here is Greek. A Trojan knows who's in the saddle.

THE KING: And that is why they must be told: Molossus shall be in the saddle.

Long pause.

AGAMEMNON: Very good. We have heard the rhetoric. Duly memorized from Pyrrhus' book. It is dangerous, or I would not have come here . . .

THE KING: Ah! So we are getting to the real reason finally!

AGAMEMNON: Right. We are getting to the real reason. Notions like Pyrrhus' present a danger. The principal danger to Greece today—and to all law and order. Which is why—whatever my view of the . . . execution—I have to be glad he is gone, Peleus. I have to be. But this is all beside the point because you are not Pyrrhus. You are an old man deprived of Pyrrhus. As before you were deprived of Achilles. (*Viciously*.) And so now: a helpless cripple left without a crutch.

THE KING: I saw a cripple once. He couldn't walk a step without his crutches. And one day, as he hobbled down the alley, the village bully grabbed his crutches from him. He fell on his face. But when bystanders ran to pick him up, he was too quick for them: got up and stalked away, propelled by rage and pride.

AGAMEMNON: And still you'll lose. Have you got that through your thick head? Strike all the splendid attitudes you want: YOU'LL STILL LOSE.

THE KING: I do not think so.

AGAMEMNON: Ha!

THE KING (*unflapped*): But I can bear the thought.

AGAMEMNON: For years, all you have done—you see, I know about you, Peleus—is dream of doing nothing, you who . . .

THE KING: Old age—you're right—should be quite differently seen. Not as sleep after toil . . . An old man has such wonderful advantages! No brilliant career to cut short, like young Orestes. No ambitions anyone can threaten, like you. There is nothing you can do to me, King Agamemnon. Which leaves me with no reason for not . . . honoring my commitment.

AGAMEMNON: Very well then, I give up. (*Goes to door by which he entered.*) This is my adjutant.

ADJUTANT *enters—played by the* STORY TELLER. AGAMEMNON *talks directly to him but so that* PELEUS *has to hear.*

Stop Orestes and Hermione in their tracks. Tell them to go straight to Argos. Tell them I tried everything. Home-truths. Lies. Bribes. Threats. Coaxing. Bullying. The man's immovable as rock. It's civil war.

The ADJUTANT *salutes and leaves.*

THE KING: You came here to . . . ?

AGAMEMNON: I saw they'd failed to reckon with you. And that this failure could be fatal. Came on here before them to . . . head you off, get you out of the way, if possible. It is not possible, is it?

THE KING: They kill my grandson, and you come on ahead to . . . toy with my feelings . . . and my fate!

AGAMEMNON: I am a politician. Despise me. You have earned the right. I shall ask nothing further of you. But there's one thing you will do—not for me but for your country.

THE KING: I do not follow.

AGAMEMNON: I will concede you're in the right. I'll concede more: that you *may* win—which Orestes and Hermione failed to see. It may be a winning formula Pyrrhus gave you . . . But being who and what you are, you will not use it. You are a man of peace. A patriot. At all costs you'll save Greece from civil war.

THE KING: You would appeal, then, to the best in me?

AGAMEMNON: Not even appeal, I simply put it to you . . .

THE KING: After the murder, the lies, and the blackmail, you simply put it to me. (*Pause.*) Save Greece from civil war yourself: you're the aggressor.

AGAMEMNON: I cannot hold Orestes back. Or my allies . . .

THE KING: Leave us. We are no longer listening.

AGAMEMNON (*desperately*): There's a truth you won't deny: YOU'RE ONE OF US. A Greek King among Greek Kings. You belong to the established order of this land. And that means something to you, doesn't it, Peleus? It means that when the chips are down, you will not ask where do we stand: you'll stand with us. Against slaves, against Trojans, against anybody . . . (*Breaks off.*) You are not listening.

THE KING: I do not need to listen: I know the language. It was mine—until you stuck your spears in Pyrrhus. *Your* spears. Not just Orestes' spears. The spears of the "established order of this land." How shall your spears, then, be my spears? How shall I ever again say *we* and include you in it? There are no limits you would not transgress. If you're a Greek, I am an African.

AGAMEMNON: Let me say one last thing . . .

THE KING (*claps his hands once for the* SERVANT *who enters at once*): Show this man out.

The SERVANT *escorts* AGAMEMNON *to the door.*

AGAMEMNON (*turning, and dropping all efforts at influencing* THE KING): I said you *may* win. If, as I still expect, you lose, Thiotis will be wiped off the map, like Troy before her.

THE KING: What Thiotis fought for will be remembered.

AGAMEMNON: Farewell. You will die quite soon.

THE KING: True. But you're not yet alive. And I am living for the first time.

STORY TELLER: And Agamemnon set out for Argos, there to join forces with Orestes and Hermione: a general mobilization order was sent on ahead by express courier. And the body of Pyrrhus was brought back to Thiotis and placed in the great public square before the people.

The body of PYRRHUS *on a bier.* THE KING *is on a dais or balcony above it. Beside him is* ANDROMACHE *with her child on a cushion.*

THE KING: People of Thiotis! We mourn Pyrrhus: my grandson and your brother. We denounce his assassins: Orestes and his hooded hatchet men, Hermione who set them on. And we denounce Agamemnon, King of Argos, accessory after the fact, conspirator against our independence, who even now's preparing to invade us. Let those who would not resist him leave, and let all who would resist —Trojan or not, slave or not—henceforth be this city's citizens. (*Pause.*) No one has left? Then let our mourning be tempered with rejoicing! In token whereof I now take this child—son of Greek Pyrrhus, Trojan Andromache— and on my sole authority declare him LEGITIMATE! (*He raises child and cushion high above his head with both hands. A trumpet sounds.*) Tomorrow, Agamemnon, and the struggle unending!

the author's apology

i. To Sophocles

Your story is so good we too much write it;
Our times so bad that we must re-enact it.
Wasn't it just last week some kid was seen
Darting in blue jeans through the darkened streets
Down to the city gates and out beyond
To give a butchered brother burial?
Where *was* that? Mississippi? Prague? Saigon?
There are Creons in the saddle East and West!
Would you not, Master, be the first to say:
To every Creon his Antigone?

ii. To Euripides

You told how this world was, and nothing's changed:
Pyrrhus has died a million deaths since your day
Slain by ten million Oresteses.
The hoodlum gets the hero every time.
And that is that? The world is run by hoodlums
Abetted by their genocidal gunmolls
And backed up by the boys who run for office?
You didn't say so: you created Peleus.
But then you sent his wife the goddess Thetis
To yank him off to Florida or someplace!
We can't accept that. Peleus has to stay
To show that things could end another way.

production notes

I have deliberately refrained from stating in the text what each of the characters looks like: this is for the stage director to decide. There are characters here who could be played equally well by a fat actor or a thin, a blond or a dark, and so on.

What clothes they should wear is again largely the director's option, but since my opinion has been asked in the past, when the plays were being produced, I will give it here. My advice to producers of these plays is: forget about Greece, especially classical Greece. In my view, there is enough of Greece in the text itself—the stories are Greek, the places and persons all have Greek names. Let what is added in production be modern, and not necessarily modern Greek. It may be replied that the Greek names prevent the play from being specifically anything non-Greek. But that, I shall retort, is the point of the method used. The setting must not be specifically one country. This is a matter not merely of stage design and costume but of the very dramaturgy. The idea of using mythology while having nothing in mind but modern subject matter is to set the modernities *at a remove* so they can be looked at critically. The life of such plays is in the analogies between the old story and modern situations. But the playwright does not limit himself to one analogy. Even if his play grew out of one crisis (in Algeria or Vietnam or wherever), he must write, if he can, so that it applies in other crises—for these other crises, until basic historical changes occur, are indeed *analogous*.

By the same token, the playwright will not stipulate Algerian or Vietnamese costume, but rather leave the director free to exploit whatever is the crisis of the hour when the play is done. Even then—to refine a suggestion just given—it will be a mistake to create a *completely* Algerian or Vietnamese drama. Neither stage design nor costume should create the milieu of just one country. It is the analogousness that is important: not that "it happened in Algeria" but that it is happening all over, or, alternatively, that it has happened in certain places and could happen here. Not only, then, must a director not limit himself to a single analogy: rather, he must try to suggest as many analogies as possible, especially analogies with whatever is seriously wrong in his own place and time.

Reverting to what the characters should look like, "any resemblance to persons living or dead is purely coincidental." No character in *A Time to Die* or in *A Time to Live* is a historical or journalistic portrait. But there are likenesses at moments, and sometimes beyond that. These, however, need not be the same for each spectator. As Creon, Arthur Hill reminded me of McGeorge Bundy, but there was no intentional mimicry in the performance, and other spectators doubtless thought of other Creons. If a Negro played Creon, some spectators would think of Roy Wilkins. And so on. If the part is written right, it will point the finger at *your* Creon for you.

The director should again "forget about Greece" when he is working with the narrators in these plays. For narrators are what they are—not Greek choruses. Directors who "forget" this are apt to have them adopt a solemn and/or melancholy tone which tends to make the plays lugubrious if not pompous and is, in any case, a misinterpretation of what is going on: the slave-narrators of the first play are *celebrating* the memory of Antigone. Their tone is one of admiration, enthusiasm, and, in the end, joy. The second play, whatever intellectual cargo it carries, is just a tale and, as such, can be followed and enjoyed by children, as I had the chance to prove with my own seven-year-olds. The actor who plays Story Teller should know this, provided that the knowledge doesn't push him too far in the other direction and cause him to adopt the silly, sing-song pseudo-infantile voice of professional readers to children. When I say the play is for children, I am not thinking of children as Little Darlings but as connoisseurs of consequent narrative—and, of course, as addicts of violence . . .

Antigone is celebrated. And Peleus is celebrated. But even celebration becomes melancholy if the emphasis is on the past, telling us that our hero is no more. The narrators should be child-like in this too, that they are oriented toward the future, the future is more real to them than the past, they are thinking of Antigones and Peleuses to come: these are stories of possibility. If we are brought up to believe that the opposite attitude is in itself nobler, then our upbringing is prejudiced. What, generally, lies behind sentiments like "Gone, all are gone, the old familiar faces"? Surely only the defeatist feeling of the self-centered middle-aged that life itself is shrinking as their friends die off.

I would commend to others an idea of Herbert Berghof's: that the body of Polynices should lie center stage throughout the action of *A Time to Die.*

It should not escape notice that an exposed and mangled corpse has an important place in *A Time to Live* as well. The designer should try to give visual expression to the difference that there is between a scoundrel slaughtered in the natural course of a war he did much to cause and a hero deliberately assassinated *by* scoundrels. Polynices, dead, is at best pitiable, since he is our brother. Pyrrhus, dead, is an inspiration and a challenge.